The Wisdom Of 40 Summers
Stories Of Grace, Grit And Growth

The Wisdom of 40 Summers: Stories Of Grace, Grit And Growth

The Wisdom Of 40 Summers
Stories Of Grace, Grit And Growth

Adeyinka Adewale PhD

The Wisdom of 40 Summers: Stories Of Grace, Grit And Growth

THE WISDOM OF 40 SUMMERS:
Stories Of Grace, Grit And Growth

Copyright © 2025 by Adeyinka Adewale
All right reserved.
ISBN: 979-8-89778-721-0

All rights reserved. No part of this publication may be reproduced, stored in a retrieval system, or transmitted in any form or by any means, electronic, mechanical, photocopying, recording, scanning, or otherwise, without the prior written permission of the author.

Designed by
Tolu Israel
toluisrael@thirteen21.one

Staten House

Adeyinka Adewale PhD
Email: yinkaadewale@yahoo.com

ISBN 979-8-89778-721-0

DEDICATION

To ImisiOluwa and IniOluwa, my precious gifts.

May the lessons within these pages serve as a compass for your journey.

May you always walk in wisdom, rise with courage, and lead with love.

You are the reason I strive, the light in my purpose, and the future I pray for daily.

Everything I've learned so far, I leave in your hands so you can stand taller, dream bolder, and walk further than I ever could.

With all my love,
Daddy

The Wisdom of 40 Summers: Stories Of Grace, Grit And Growth

TABLE OF CONTENTS

Acknowledgments vii

Foreword viii

Preface x

Chapter 1: Origins, Choices and Perspectives 1

Chapter 2: Journey into Excellence 18

Chapter 3: From Triumph to Defeat – And Back Again 34

Chapter 4: Right People, Right Information, Right Time 55

Chapter 5: Carpe Diem! Seize the Moment! 74

Chapter 6: More Wins, More Possibilities 89

Chapter 7: God's Crucible 108

Chapter 8: The Darkest Hours and The Triumph of Faith 131

Chapter 9: Moulding Lives, Building Nations:
    A Life of Purpose and Service 149

Chapter 10: Driven by Legacy 169

40 Wisdom Keys for Life 184

ACKNOWLEDGEMENTS

This book is a reflection of many voices, sacrifices, and moments that shaped my journey. I am deeply grateful to God, the ultimate Author of my story, whose grace has carried me through every season.

To my wife, Oluwabamike — your love, strength, and unwavering support continue to steady and inspire me. You are my answered prayer and daily gift.

To my parents, whose resilience and vision laid the foundation for so much of who I am — thank you.

To my siblings, extended family, mentors, pastors, friends, teachers, Church family and guides who poured wisdom into my path, thank you for believing in me before I believed in myself. This book carries your fingerprints.

And to the readers — thank you for holding these words in your hands and heart. May they meet you where you are and remind you that your journey matters.

FOREWORD

There are books you read and then there are books that read you. The Wisdom of 40 Summers is the latter. It speaks to the soul, reaches into the heart, and calls you to reflect, realign, and rise. With each page, you're invited into a sacred conversation about life, legacy, and the lessons that truly matter. In a world obsessed with instant results and surface-level success, Adeyinka Adewale offers something rare: depth, authenticity, and perspective. This is not a collection of catchy slogans or borrowed ideas. It is a well of wisdom drawn from a life lived with intention, faith, and resilience.

What makes this work truly remarkable is that it isn't just written, it's lived. Adeyinka doesn't write as a distant observer; he speaks as a fellow traveller. With honesty and humility, he shares the moments that shaped him—the triumphs, the trials, the tears, and the turning points. His story is not a tale of survival but a testimony of transformation and proof of what happens when a man dares to believe God's version of his life.

Over the years, I've had the privilege of walking closely with Adeyinka. I've watched him rise from quiet beginnings, wrestle through seasons of uncertainty, and emerge with clarity, courage, and character. I've seen him embody a rare blend of grace and grit, strength and surrender. His journey has not been perfect, but it has been purposeful and now, he offers the wisdom gained through four decades as a gift to the world.

This book is deeply personal, yet profoundly universal. It doesn't shout, it speaks. It doesn't impress, it imparts. And in doing so, it meets you where you are whether you're just starting out or standing at a crossroads. Through stories, insights, and timeless truths, it gently guides you to ask the right questions, reflect on your own journey, and chart a course with faith and clarity.

The Wisdom of 40 Summers won't promise you quick fixes but it will give you lasting principles. If you take them to heart, they will help you see more clearly, live more intentionally, and lead more purposefully. It has been a great honour to mentor Adeyinka Adewale to pour into him, and now to witness him pour into others through this work. His voice carries weight. His words hold wisdom and this book has a message that will bless your life.

Rev. Dr. Sam Oye
Founder & Lead Pastor, The Transforming Church
CEO, Springtime Leadership Consult
Host, Prophetic Prayer Hour

PREFACE

Life is a collection of seasons, each bringing its lessons, challenges, and triumphs. Some seasons break us, others build us, but all of them shape us. This book is a reflection of my journey through four decades - 40 summers filled with experiences that have taught me the invaluable lessons of grace, grit, and growth.

As I look back on my life, I see a pattern: every struggle refined me, every victory expanded my vision, and every challenge stretched my capacity to become more. From unexpected entrepreneurial ventures to life-changing moments of faith, from academic achievements to bold leaps into the unknown, each experience carried a wisdom key that unlocked greater possibilities.

This book is not just my story; it is an invitation for you to reflect on your own. With each chapter, I share defining moments from my journey, distilling powerful wisdom keys that have shaped my life. Across ten chapters, you will find 40 transformative insights, and practical principles that can help you navigate your path, embrace challenges, and discover the power of resilience, faith, and continuous growth.

The Wisdom of 40 Summers is more than a memoir, it is a guide, a conversation, and a mirror that will encourage you to see the lessons in your own experiences. I hope that as you turn these pages, you will not only gain wisdom but also find the courage to embrace life with a renewed perspective. I encourage you to reflect, engage, and apply. May these stories remind you that every win, every challenge, and every step forward is a building block for something greater. And above all, may you discover that the best is always yet to come.

Let's journey together.

Adeyinka Adewale, PhD

CHAPTER ONE

Origins, Choices and Perspectives

"Two roads diverged in a wood, and I took the one less travelled by, And that has made all the difference."

- Robert Frost.

I came into this world on a Monday in Ibadan, the largest indigenous city in West Africa by land area. My father had hoped I would arrive on Sunday, April 28, 1985, just in time before he travelled to the United Kingdom later that day. The day started with the anticipation of my arrival, but as it became apparent that there was no sign of labour, my mum encouraged my dad to catch his flight. By 7 p.m., my father had to make a difficult decision to leave for the airport in Lagos, a city about 120 kilometres away to make his 11 p.m. flight. Upon his arrival in London six hours later, he telephoned and got the news that I had arrived at exactly 1 am.

I became my mother's sixth son and my father's fifth. The midwife who delivered me was claimed to have said "It's another boy, oh!" Her tone carried a mix of familiarity and finality as if subtly warning my mother to give up any hope of a daughter lest she end up with a seventh son. But life has its ironies. Three years later in another Southern Nigerian city, another woman was expecting a child - her tenth baby. To imagine having ten children in today's world might seem overwhelming, but for her, it was her reality. In September 1988, she gave birth once again to another daughter. That tenth daughter would one day become the woman I love and call my wife.

The mathematics of these births are astounding. The probability of having 10 girls in 10 pregnancies from the same woman is roughly 1 in 1024 (0.0976%), less than a one per cent chance. Equally fascinating, my mother's probability of having six boys in six pregnancies was approximately 1 in 64 (1.563%). The numbers make it clear - neither I nor my wife were statistical probabilities; we were divine appointments. And if we take this further considering the probability of me being the one sperm cell out of millions to fertilize the egg that formed me, it only deepens my conviction: I was not a mistake. I was meant to be.

But this was only the beginning of a greater story.

Culture, Religion, and the Complexities of Family

I opened my eyes on this side of eternity and found myself surrounded by a loving but complex family. As the last-born, one might assume I was pampered endlessly, but that wasn't exactly the case. While I was well cared for, my upbringing was not one of indulgence but of structured care, discipline, and a blend of affection and tough love. In the innocence of childhood, I saw family as a single, cohesive unit, parents, siblings, warmth, and laughter. But as my awareness grew, I quickly learned that family is not always simple. It can be exciting, enriching, and deeply comforting, yet it can also be tricky, complicated, and, at times, tense.

It took me years to fully grasp that brothers and sisters don't always share both parents, and that love alone is what truly defines family. Around the age of four, I discovered that I had other siblings in Lagos, children from my father's first marriage. My mother was his second wife, and the first wife had five children who were much older than my siblings and I. Looking back now, I must give my father his due credit. Managing two homes in two different cities while remaining present and engaged was no small feat. Yet, he did it effortlessly. He travelled to be with us every weekend for as long as I can remember, and when he wasn't physically present, he called every other day, checking in on us, school and general well-being. It was only in hindsight that I understood the immense commitment this required - he truly was a super dad.

Yet, this family dynamic left me with many questions. I remember asking my school friends, "Does your daddy have another family elsewhere?" as though I was searching for someone who shared my reality, another child who, like me, was navigating this unique family setup. My question was often met with confused looks, and for a long time, I thought I was the only one with such a story. It wasn't until later that I met a classmate or two who also came from polygamous homes and were still processing that reality.

To be clear, polygamy was not an unusual concept in the society I was born into. In Yoruba culture, historically, a man could marry as many wives as his wealth permitted, it was a status symbol, a marker of prosperity. However, the intersection of culture and religion created further complexities. If you were born into a Muslim family, polygamy was generally accepted, as it aligned with religious doctrine. But in Christian homes, monogamy was expected yet, cultural influences meant that even among Christians, there were men who had multiple wives. This contradiction made for a confusing reality. My father belonged to the silent generation - men who upheld tradition with as much devotion as they did their religious beliefs. Their worldview was shaped by a deep respect for culture, an unshakable commitment to providing for their families, and a firm belief in the importance of legacy. So, it wasn't surprising that aspects of the culture they subscribed to were held unto as religiously as whichever faith they practised. Some also remained core traditionalists even in their religious practices.

In another twist to this family plot, I also then found out that three of my brothers whom I had become very fond of and loved deeply were fathered by another man, not my father. My mother was in her second marriage after a failed first one that produced three sons. Reflecting on how close I was at that tender age with my brothers, it could have only been because my father had accepted them and raised us all as his own. To him, they were simply his sons - no prefixes, no conditions and my father's commitment to them was the same. That was how I came to see all my brothers. Education was his greatest priority. He firmly believed that quality education was the best legacy a parent could give their child. He lived by this conviction, funding the education of not just his children but also his nieces, nephews, and many extended family members all of whom he became responsible for. Growing up in such an intricate family setup surrounded by loving uncles, aunties from both sides and my maternal grandmother whom I grew very fond of showed me how love removes differences. We were simply one big family, yet imagine the mind of a young four to six-year-old boy making these discoveries and attempting to make sense of his world. It was a lot to process.

But not all was seamless. The love between my dad's 'two families' was not always cordial. There were tensions, unspoken but ever-present. There was no outright hostility, at least to my best recollection, but there was an undercurrent of not being liked by the other side. Moreover, whenever we had a large family gathering at our family home in Oyo town, we were instructed on how to conduct ourselves. My mother would sit us down and emphasize rules like: Do not eat anything unless I approve it; Be cautious with gifts; Declare everything you receive before accepting it; Watch what you say and how you act and so on. As a child who just wanted to enjoy life, being taught this level of caution at that age was life-changing. It meant coming to a realisation that not everyone in your life has your best interest at heart. It felt like walking on eggshells having to navigate my family dynamics with caution. This was my first lesson in guardedness. It was a difficult lesson for a child to learn, but given the context, it was a necessary one.

At times, I struggled with it. There were days I wished I had been born into a different family, a simpler one. Yet, in time, I realized that my family story, though complex, was a masterclass in human relationships. As the philosopher Viktor Frankl once wrote in Man's Search for Meaning:

"Everything can be taken from a man but one thing: the last of the human freedoms—to choose one's attitude in any given set of circumstances."

It took me twenty years to embrace this wisdom and activate this power of choice. While I cannot control the circumstances into which I was born, I can control the perspectives I adopt and the actions I take. This is often where growth lies and when I became more conscious of this truth, it changed how I viewed my past - and shaped the way I approach my future.

Choices and perspectives shape our realities.

The guardedness I had become used to had also gradually morphed into a silent but potent fear the older I got - 'you don't know who is out to get you'. It became a default way of thinking to the extent that it fostered a sense of 'helplessness' and a feeling that life's outcomes are almost always outside of one's control. At its extremes, it meant that if one failed an exam, it would be because there were 'evil forces' from one's household responsible for that failure and not a person's lack of preparedness or other possible factors. It also becomes convenient to blame these forces rather than take responsibility for one's actions. This is not to disregard the reality of evil forces and their possibility of influencing a person's outcomes negatively in life. I have lived to see this to be true in many instances, but there was a toxic outlook to life and a crippling helplessness that becomes an individual's default perspective with this type of mindset. Grappling with this formed worldview would become a huge part of my initial struggles as I began to step into adulthood. Nothing else changed until I dealt with this settled state of thinking.

I started experiencing a turning point when I was about the age of eighteen after completing my secondary education and was attempting to get into the university. Certain key discoveries in that season gave me the keys that helped steer my life away from my previous default victimhood mentality into a more positive, empowering one. My father had the grand idea to take me away from Ibadan where I had grown up and schooled all my life, also where my mum lived to Lagos where he lived and worked with my stepmum. His vision was for me to attend the University of Lagos which eventually materialised but he also wanted me to be under his direct supervision. I was very hesitant and loathed the idea at first but had no choice. I moved to Lagos a sore and scared young man. My thinking constantly focused on thoughts like, "Why should this have to be me?", "How will this end?" amongst others. I was scared I might not do well and my fears were driven by the guardedness that had evolved into a victim mentality. I was lost in the cocoon of my myopia. My first months were rough, trying to hide and not to be seen too much. I would stay for long hours in my little office beside my dad's office to avoid any confrontation with my stepmum. But as time progressed, this was not realistic. I was plunged into the full flow of being a part of the house and that was when I began to notice the interplay of three forces – perspectives, choices and outcomes.

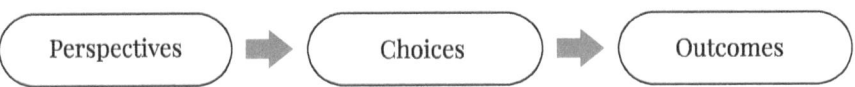

Figure 1.1: Perspectives – Choices – Outcome Model 1

I began to understand that my perspectives shape my choices, and those choices ultimately define my outcomes, as illustrated in the figure above. Initially, this relationship seemed straightforward: perspective influences outcomes directly through choices. Gradually, though, I recognized just how powerful perspective is in determining the choices we make. All it takes to shift our viewpoint is allowing new information to challenge our previous assumptions. Sometimes, even a slight adjustment in perspective can trigger profound transformations. To grasp the potency of this idea, imagine yourself driving along a straight road. If you steer the wheel slightly - just by one degree - to the right or left, can you visualize what happens? The entire car shifts direction significantly over time. The difference between staying on course and veering off track often comes down to a minor tilt and mere seconds.

This powerful insight crystallized for me when I read three impactful books. The first two, "As a Man Thinketh" by James Allen, an original copy I still cherish today, and "Men of Purpose" by Peter Masters were gifts from my dad. The third was

"Gifted Hands" by Ben Carson, recommended by one of my university professors. I saved diligently to purchase this book myself. I hadn't even finished the first five pages of "As a Man Thinketh" before clearly recognizing the root cause of my limitations and bitterness: my thinking. If I could change my thoughts, I could change my life. Altering my thinking would enable me to overcome adversity, reshape my vision, transform my actions, and ultimately create different outcomes. The ripple effect of this realization was monumental for my 18-year-old self.

Two years later, when I finally got hold of "Gifted Hands," my understanding deepened further. I began to see that the relationship among perspectives, choices, and outcomes might be far more complex than I'd initially thought. Instead of a simple linear sequence, it resembled more closely the intricate two-way feedback loop system depicted below:

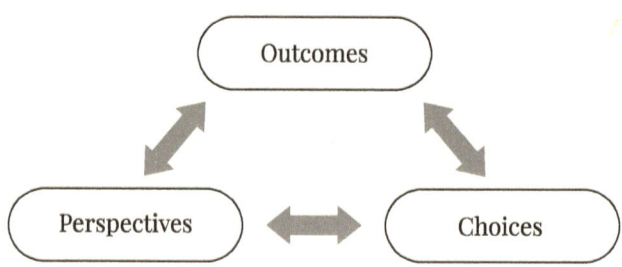

Figure 1.2: Perspectives – Choices – Outcome Model 2

All three components interact and influence each other profoundly, making it challenging to escape cycles of negative thinking. Let's explore this more deeply. Perspectives shape choices, but choices, in turn, influence perspectives. For example, if I believe the world is against me, I might choose to behave defensively or negatively, reflecting that very perspective. Once a choice is made, we instinctively seek evidence to confirm it, further reinforcing our initial viewpoint - a phenomenon known as confirmation bias.

In my case, stories I heard about the experiences of others and my extreme guardedness conditioned my perspective, influencing my subsequent choices. Each time I acted on those choices, I subconsciously searched for attitudes, actions, and behaviours from others that validated my views. Consequently, adopting this perspective directly impacted my outcomes, and these outcomes, in turn, either reinforced or challenged my perspectives. Processing the feedback from outcomes objectively and without bias is essential, yet difficult, especially once our perspective has become entrenched. I had convinced myself that my immediate environment wasn't conducive to my growth. This belief risked becoming an excuse for failure, justifying setbacks simply because of where I lived. Indeed, I was heading down that path. The relationship between choices and outcomes works similarly; every choice has a consequence, and these outcomes can either validate or challenge our initial decisions. However, biases can blind us to vital signals necessary for meaningful change.

I came to understand that of these three components, perspective, choices, and outcomes—the most powerful was perspective. It was the foundational element that had to shift for everything else to align. If my choices didn't match my true perspective, it was likely due to external pressures compromising my free will. To achieve lasting transformation, my worldview had to fundamentally change, beginning with how I interpreted my circumstances. This realization is precisely why books had such a profound impact on me.

The balance among these three elements shifted dramatically for me when I read Men of Purpose, a book detailing the inspiring life stories of some of history's most remarkable inventors and entrepreneurs. I remember being captivated by the stories of Heinz's beginnings and Michael Faraday's groundbreaking discoveries. None of these influential figures achieved greatness effortlessly; each overcame significant challenges along the way.

Soon after, Gifted Hands, the remarkable story of Ben Carson impacted my thinking. Carson's journey from an impoverished childhood in a single-parent home to international acclaim as a paediatric neurosurgeon resonated deeply with me. I couldn't put the book down. Within its pages, I saw reflections of myself and glimpses of the person I aspired to become - a globally respected professional in whatever path I chose. This pivotal moment transformed my perspective forever. If Ben Carson could achieve such greatness, so could I.

My perspectives began to shift, replacing my habitual negative question, "What's the worst that could happen here?" with a more empowering one, "What's the greatest achievement I can reach while I'm here?" This slight yet significant shift in thinking profoundly changed my outlook and aspirations. I began to dream boldly and without reservation. Internally, I felt myself transforming. I replaced the narrative of a hostile world with the empowering idea that everyone, knowingly or unknowingly, was contributing positively to my future success. Nights became opportunities to daydream the future I deeply desired, bringing it into clearer focus. It was during this transformative period that I wrote in my diary the specific achievements I wished to attain. I could not dream big and well until I experienced this shift. This chapter in my life elevated me beyond the limited perceptions I'd previously held about my family and my circumstances, profoundly reshaping my vision of what was possible.

Changing my perspective reversed years of negative thinking and conditioning. I realized my life was far more within my control than I'd ever believed, and that I had given others too much power to influence me negatively. Yet, this refinement in thinking is essential for growth and maturity. Another profound lesson from that period was that true growth required stepping out of my comfort zone. I often reflect on how different my life would have been had I never left the comfort of living with my mum in Ibadan. I didn't choose my family, yet they remain the foundation upon which my story is built. Since my beginnings were beyond my control, I consider them sacred. Our origins shape our perspectives, bringing both limitations and blessings. However, the responsibility for transforming ourselves, for experiencing a rebirth in mindset and purpose, ultimately rests with us. I am profoundly grateful to God for revealing this truth early enough to shape the man I was to become.

Those formative years with my father were pivotal. His steadfast principles of integrity, diligence, responsibility, and service were more than mere lessons—they represented my rite of passage from childhood into manhood. I've learned that everything we encounter in life, whether beautiful or painful, can serve a divine purpose if we choose to see it that way. I say this with great humility and sensitivity to readers whose experiences, particularly regarding family, may have been challenging.

What followed was a series of life-changing encounters and events that reshaped me profoundly, events I'll explore further in the coming chapters. But let's be clear about one thing: Perspective is incredibly powerful. It shapes how we interpret our past and envision our future. Perspective transforms our challenges into stepping stones instead of stumbling blocks. As James Allen wrote in As a Man Thinketh, *"You are today where your thoughts have brought you; you will be tomorrow where your thoughts take you."*

May we all have the courage to choose love, the wisdom to embrace perspective, and the faith to trust in the divine plan that ultimately makes all things beautiful in their own time.

Wisdom Keys from Chapter 1

1. Circumstances Do Not Define Us, Our Choices Do

While we do not choose the families or conditions we are born into, we have the power to shape our lives through the choices we make. My journey illustrates that even in complex family dynamics, one can rise above challenges through intentional choices.

2. Perspective Determines Reality

The shift in mindset from focusing on limitations to embracing possibilities was a turning point. A change in perspective, choosing to see every experience as a contributor to growth, can redefine our lives and open doors to greater opportunities.

3. Adversity is a Catalyst for Growth

The discomfort of leaving a familiar environment and adapting to new circumstances became the foundation for transformation. Growth often requires stepping out of our comfort zones and embracing the unknown with courage.

4. The Power of Thought Shapes Destiny

The lesson from *As a Man Thinketh and Gifted Hands* revealed that thoughts dictate outcomes. The decision to envision a brighter future, despite past difficulties, led to a renewed sense of purpose and ambition. As James Allen puts it, "You are today where your thoughts have brought you; you will be tomorrow where your thoughts take you."

Reflection Questions

1. How have your early experiences shaped your perspective on life?

Reflect on the lessons and narratives you inherited from your upbringing. Are they empowering you, or do they need to be reframed for growth?

2. What limiting beliefs are holding you back from fully embracing your potential?

Identify thoughts or mindsets that may be preventing you from seeing opportunities in adversity. How can you shift your thinking to a more empowering perspective?

3. What is one choice you can make today that will positively impact your future?

Every major transformation begins with a single decision. What action can you take now to move closer to the person you aspire to be?

CHAPTER TWO

Journey into Excellence

"We are what we repeatedly do. Excellence, then, is not an act, but a habit."

- Aristotle.

I find concrete work intriguing. When I moved to Lagos, part of my responsibility was to become an unpaid intern in my dad's private land surveying practice. I was expected to handle various tasks and frequently had to acquire new skills along the way. Concrete work soon became a significant part of my job. Whenever clients approached my father to demarcate their land boundaries and draft survey plans, our initial step involved using exact coordinates and a Global Positioning System (GPS) to locate existing pillars on site. Often, we spent hours searching the coordinates, only to find old, eroded concrete stubs that needed to be restored. This required either installing entirely new pillars or adding fresh concrete caps with newly assigned numbers to existing stubs buried underground.

My first real experience with concrete came during one of these projects. I vividly recall the day my dad tasked me and a junior surveyor to produce about 30 pillar caps for a large-scale project.

Each cap was a square concrete slab about four inches thick, and they needed to meet precise quality standards. We followed detailed guidelines outlining the exact proportions of cement, sharp sand, and water, mixing them by hand before pouring the concrete into wooden moulds of a standard size. Initially, the mixture was wet and soft, easy to mould. However, once it began to dry and harden, it became impossible to reshape without significant effort, such as using a hammer and chisel.

One particular step required careful timing: stamping numbers onto each cap. If we attempted this too soon while the concrete was still wet, it would become messy and illegible. If we waited too long, the concrete would be too hardened for stamping. The timing was critical, and a brief half-hour window provided the perfect conditions for the task. This experience deeply impressed upon me the importance of timing, ease, and recognizing the right seasons in life. In Proverbs 6:6-8, Scripture instructs us to observe the ants, learn from their wisdom, and apply it to our lives. What wisdom can ants possibly teach us? The passage explains that even without commanders or rulers, ants diligently gather and store food during the favourable seasons, knowing that difficult times will inevitably come. They don't wait for winter to start preparing; by then, it would be too late. Ants instinctively grasp the importance of timing, preparation, and diligence.

This principle applies equally to life. Every task has its perfect timing, and missing that timing can lead to severe, often irreversible consequences. When you possess the strength, energy, and resources, do not delay—what feels easy now might become exceedingly difficult or even impossible later. Building discipline in the right season equips you for future challenges. At this stage of my journey, I began to understand the immense value of developing good habits early enough to ensure a successful future. Had I missed that crucial season, my story could have unfolded very differently.

Reflecting on this journey, I recognize that being taught to embrace diligence by my father from a young age allowed me to effortlessly cultivate this essential value at precisely the right season. This foundation significantly impacted my life, and its roots will be explored more deeply in subsequent chapters. At just ten years old, I began to realize the immense benefits of this early discipline -benefits that continue to shape who I am today.

A Foundation of Diligence

As soon as I could speak and have intelligent conversations with an adult, my parents began to instil key disciplines and values into my siblings and I. The most cogent ones were integrity, diligence and excellence. The mantra for integrity was simply that 'a good name is better than silver and gold'. For diligence, it was 'a slothful man would never get anything done' and for excellence, 'whatever is worth doing at all is worth doing well'. It was during this time also that my father taught me the power of diligence. If I had taken count of the number of times he said to my siblings and I, "You have to work hard", it could have been more than a million times. In fact whenever I did something wrong or did not achieve a set objective and he invited me to reflect on what had happened – that is another thing my father made me do frequently – to think and reflect on events or outcomes, my default answer was always, "I did not work hard enough".

As a youngster, he sounded like a broken record but he had his way. He would ensure that we had an early start to our day and work us late into the night whenever he could. His method of instilling diligence in us included an agreed daily dose of household chores – we lived in a fairly big house with a big compound. Quality control of everything was quite a thing and this was the only way to guarantee excellence. At times, I had to sweep the living room and some exterior parts of the house. Whenever I swept, my father would take off his shoes and drag his feet around the swept area to spot any upswept patches. I knew I was about to be asked to sweep that floor all over again if he found any bits not well done. Whenever there was a plumbing problem, my father would rather attempt to mend it with my siblings and I acting as his assistants. We had a storeroom with a massive wooden box of tools of all sorts to enable all of our repair adventures in the house. If it wasn't repairs, it would be cleaning and laundry or cooking in the kitchen. We were engaged on the domestic front. His philosophy was clear, discipline is acquired from active participation in the home economy and diligence was expected across all key areas of function. The only thing we were not allowed to worry about was provision for our subsistence.

On the academic front, my father was a stickler for excellence. He would assign portions of assignments to my brothers and I in various subjects which he looked over every weekend when he returned from his workstation in Lagos. In instances where he wasn't satisfied with the work done, he would get me to stay back late into the night to work on sums or any piece of work that had to be done. It felt very cruel and unreasonable but he was programming grit into my system. All I wanted to do was play and have fun. But as I grew older I understood the gift he had given to me – the gift of work and a strong work ethic. As much as I disliked his methods, and my personality type encouraged me to enjoy playing and leaving important things until later, I had no choice but to comply. But as it is with unpleasant situations, once we are exposed to the benefits that they carry, then they make sense.

The realization of this hit me profoundly when my father's insistence on excellence and diligence propelled me into the realm of historic academic achievement. I was just ten years old. This period was particularly significant, as it coincided with my personal decision to follow Jesus - a choice I made independently, not influenced by my parents. At the time, I was in my sixth year of primary school and had become the Head Boy, which indicated I wasn't doing badly academically. My leadership qualities were evident, matched by solid academic performance, consistently placing me among the top ten students in my class.

As preparations began for both public and private secondary school examinations, my father adopted a structured approach.

He required me to methodically work through all my subjects textbooks from cover to cover. His philosophy was straightforward - he expected me to thoroughly master every problem presented in the textbooks. Together, we set weekly targets of completing one or two mathematics chapters, alongside assignments in English and other key subjects. One weekend afternoon, during one of our usual conversations, he suddenly asked, "Do you know Pythagoras theorem?" I can't recall exactly how we reached that topic, but I distinctly remember my surprise. "Pytha…what? What is that?" I thought, feeling immediately anxious. I began to worry that I might be headed for another late-night study session if this was something I was already supposed to know. Sheepishly, I answered, "No, Sir."

He sat me down patiently, explaining the theorem clearly, using examples and making me repeat it repeatedly until I understood it fully. My father, who was skilled in mathematics through his background as a physicist and professional land surveyor, excelled at guiding us through complex concepts. When he asked me to bring out my textbook, we discovered, to my great relief, that Pythagoras' theorem was covered much later in the advanced chapters. However, for reasons known only to him, he insisted that I learn it right away, and so I did, diligently mastering the theorem that weekend.

Pythagoras Theorem for the win

The following week at school, my class teacher stepped into our classroom one afternoon and made an exciting announcement. The Federal Government of Nigeria had decided to award mathematics scholarships to exceptional primary school students nationwide who were transitioning to secondary education. The selection process required top schools from each state to nominate just one student who would compete at the state level. From there, national winners would be chosen. To kick-start this selection, an impromptu mathematics test was immediately announced and set for that very afternoon. My teacher had already selected a few brilliant students from my class, including me, to participate in this unexpected competition. I clearly remember being moved into another classroom, where we joined pupils from other classes for the test.

When I received the test paper, my eyes widened in disbelief. There were twenty questions, and astonishingly, every single one was about Pythagoras' theorem! I felt a rush of emotions- shock, excitement, and confusion - all at once. How could it be possible that I had just learned this exact topic over the weekend with my father, and now it would determine who represented our school at a national level? It felt surreal, almost magical. Steadying my nerves, I calmly worked through the questions, confidently handed in my paper, and left the room. My classmates stared in amazement, as many of them genuinely struggled with the challenging questions that fate had seemingly placed in my path.

After returning to my class, about six of us who had taken the test gathered anxiously around the blackboard to review our solutions. Among them were two friends of mine who were particularly gifted in mathematics. I had assumed the test would be easy for them, but to my astonishment, they struggled to find the right answers. After several unsuccessful attempts, I stepped forward, picked up a piece of chalk, calmly explained the theorem, and solved the problem. My class teacher watched in delight and confirmed that my solution was correct.

The next morning, it was announced that I had scored a perfect 100%, making me the chosen representative for the school at the state competition. You would think this news filled me with joy, but instead, anxiety and self-doubt flooded my mind. I felt like an imposter, convinced I didn't truly deserve this opportunity and terrified that I might embarrass myself on a bigger stage. Yet, I had no choice but to accept the nomination. When my father called from Lagos later that day, I shared the news. He expressed cautious excitement but quickly reminded me that representing the school carried immense responsibility. I would need to dedicate myself seriously to preparation. Over the following weeks, with the help of my siblings, I studied intensely and practised numerous mathematics tests under strictly timed conditions.

On the day of the exam, one of my brothers accompanied me to the venue. This exam was solely dedicated to mathematics. When I stepped into the examination hall, I was overwhelmed by the sight of about two hundred students from various schools, each determined to stand out on the national stage.

Honestly, I didn't fancy my chances. I quietly resolved to do my best but had already convinced myself not to expect too much.

Seeing the sheer number of competitors, doubts filled my mind. A nagging voice reminded me, "This is just your state, imagine all the others across the country!" I hardly recall how I managed to complete that exam. Afterwards, stepping out briefly to grab a drink, my brother, who had glanced at the questions, curiously asked how I'd tackled one particular problem. Without hesitation, I replied honestly, "I don't know, I can't remember." The test was genuinely challenging. Returning to school later, I couldn't shake the feeling that perhaps someone else was more deserving of this opportunity.

The Huge Payout

About six weeks later, I was called into the principal's office. A letter had arrived for me via the school office. With a mix of curiosity and apprehension, I walked in and was handed the envelope. The principal encouraged me to open it right away. We had all been expecting correspondence regarding the results of the state-level tests, but I wasn't hopeful. Then, to my utter shock, the letter announced that I had won the National Mathematics Scholarship.

"How? What's going on?" My mind raced with questions.

In a separate envelope, a certificate confirmed my achievement, along with a promise that the first three years of my secondary education would be fully funded by the Federal Government of Nigeria. That was the day my life changed. That was the day I tasted the rewards of diligence and excellence. That was the day everything my father had been trying to instil in us finally made sense. When I brought the certificate home, my mother was overwhelmed with joy. She shouted, prayed, and celebrated in a way I had never seen before. I had not until that time ever achieved such an academic milestone. For the first time, I was recognized in a big way, not for anything else but for being brilliant. My brothers had always been my support, but this moment was mine.

When my father returned that weekend, I eagerly showed him my certificate, expecting a moment of shared pride. Instead, his response was measured, even cold: "You better keep doing your work so you don't let yourself down." It wasn't what I wanted to hear as a child, but looking back, I understand it now. He was challenging me to do more, to be more. He had shown me what was possible when one committed to diligence and focus. The rest was up to me.

As I grew older and became drawn to the world of sports, I studied athletes who had reached the highest level of mastery. I watched highlight reels of legends – Lebron James, Kobe Bryant, Michael Jordan, Lionel Messi, Cristiano Ronaldo, Serena Williams and realized that beyond talent, they all had one defining trait: an unmatched work ethic. Kobe Bryant was known to arrive at the gym as early as 3 a.m. to shoot a thousand shots before practice even started. Talent is a gift, but it is never enough. I learned quickly that: "Talent may give you a head start, but discipline gives you the home run."

Diligence is a profound catalyst for excellence - quietly powerful and consistently transformative. It goes beyond mere persistence or repetitive effort, representing instead thoughtful consistency, focused practice, and an unwavering commitment to improvement. Throughout life's journey, diligence repeatedly proves itself as the critical link connecting potential to genuine excellence. Looking back at my experiences, the direct connection between diligence and excellence becomes crystal clear. The casual yet focused effort spent mastering Pythagoras' theorem with my father prepared me to excel unexpectedly during the impromptu mathematics test at school. Likewise, diligently practising mathematics questions under timed conditions with my siblings turned initial anxiety into a readiness to perform effectively on the demanding state-level exam.

Diligence doesn't merely exist as an isolated trait; it fosters and strengthens other invaluable qualities essential for achieving excellence. It instils discipline, ensuring focused effort even when motivation wanes. It encourages humility by teaching us to recognize the value of continual learning and improvement. Patience grows naturally from diligent practice, enabling us to navigate setbacks gracefully, while resilience emerges through the disciplined habit of persistent effort. The rewards of diligence are significant and far-reaching, extending well beyond immediate academic achievements. It grants us the confidence to face life's challenges head-on, transforming potential into meaningful success. Ultimately, diligence provides the foundation upon which true excellence is built, enriching our lives and empowering us to realize our fullest capabilities.

These lessons have stayed with me.

Wisdom Keys from Chapter 2

1. Timing is Everything
Just like the concrete caps needed to be stamped at the right moment, not too soon and not too late, opportunities in life also have optimal timing. Acting at the right time can yield the best results, while hesitation or delay can make progress much harder or even impossible.

2. Diligence is a Pathway to Excellence
The rigorous discipline instilled by my father, from household chores to academic rigour, proved invaluable in shaping a strong work ethic. Excellence is rarely accidental; it is a product of consistent diligence and commitment to doing things well.

3. Success happens when Preparation Meets Opportunity
The unexpected Pythagoras theorem test proved that preparation can transform luck into success. What seemed like a random study session turned out to be the very key to winning a scholarship. Success often comes to those who prepare even when they don't see immediate results.

4. Hard Work Outlasts Talent
While talent provides an advantage, discipline and hard work are what sustain success. Just like elite athletes who put in extra effort behind the scenes, those who commit to mastering their craft will eventually outshine those who rely on talent alone.

Reflection Questions

1. What habits are you cultivating today that will prepare you for future opportunities?
Consider the skills, disciplines, and mindset you are developing. Are they positioning you for success when an unexpected opportunity arises?

2. How do you respond to hard work and discipline?
Do you see them as burdens or as tools for achieving excellence? Reflect on a time when diligence paid off in your life.

3. Are there any areas in your life where you are delaying action because you believe there's more time?
Think about decisions, projects, or goals where you might be waiting too long. What would happen if you act now?

CHAPTER THREE

From Triumph to Defeat – And Back Again

"Success is not final, failure is not fatal: it is the courage to continue that counts."

- Winston Churchill

I remember watching a compelling documentary on Netflix about the Boston Red Sox, a baseball team that experienced both incredible triumphs and heart-wrenching defeats. For decades, the Red Sox endured painful near-misses, their promising seasons often ending in disappointment and leaving their passionate fans heartbroken. Yet, against all odds, they demonstrated an extraordinary ability to rise from those crushing setbacks, turning past failures into powerful lessons that ultimately propelled them back to victory. Their remarkable comeback story resonated deeply with me, mirroring my journey of facing setbacks, wrestling with self-doubt, and finding the inner strength to persevere. Just like the Red Sox, I discovered that triumph and defeat are simply parts of a larger journey—one where diligence, resilience, and determination can guide us back from defeat toward even greater victories.

From the moment I was announced as the winner of the

National Mathematics Scholarship, something profound shifted within me. My thinking, attitude, and even my very nature seemed to change. Academic excellence became an obsession. It felt as though the lessons my father had tirelessly imparted finally took permanent root, making the idea of not excelling inconceivable to me. I began to understand deeply that success isn't just an outcome; it's fundamentally a mindset. Once nurtured, it makes winning feel natural. My first three years of high school were spent at Bodija International College—the secondary extension of my primary school—and were fully sponsored by the Federal Government. During those formative years, I was relentless, and determined to establish myself among the top students in my cohort. My identity became synonymous with academic success; everyone knew me as "the scholarship guy," and I carried that title proudly.

My friends and I often found ourselves engaged in spirited mathematics competitions, each of us vying eagerly for intellectual dominance. It was astonishing to think how quickly I'd transformed from merely getting by academically to being involved in exhilarating academic rivalries. My reputation as a scholar grew so significantly that, even as a junior secondary student, I was appointed to a school-wide prefect position—an honour unprecedented at the time. Both my leadership abilities and academic strengths were recognized and celebrated.

I recall the first time my intellectual complacency cost me dearly. Having crowned myself a mathematics prodigy, I gradually began to neglect diligent study. Overwhelming confidence convinced me I had mastered whatever topic we discussed in class, so I stopped practising regularly and took studying lightly. Then, one afternoon, my maths teacher surprised us with an impromptu test. Initially confident, my heart sank as I read the questions. For the first time in a long while, I felt completely lost. I managed to complete the test, knowing deep down that I hadn't performed well. The disappointment hit me hard—I felt I'd let myself down terribly. Worse, I dreaded the humiliation of others discovering that the celebrated maths scholarship recipient had stumbled in his strongest subject.

When the results were released, I scored the lowest among my closest friends, becoming an unexpected subject of ridicule. Though it hurt deeply, I eventually snapped out of it, absorbing a crucial lesson about the power of continuity. Ironically, I had forgotten that my initial success with Pythagoras' theorem—my claim to fame—had come from diligent practice, even when I wasn't intellectually ready by my standards. This humbling experience reinforced that the disciplines and consistent habits that lead to success must be maintained if one is to sustain it. It was an essential reminder about the principle of continuity.

Rising to a new challenge

After three successful years at my first high school, I moved to a new school—Oritamefa Baptist Model School. Immediately, I realized it was much larger and more competitive than any school I'd previously attended. Suddenly, I found myself surrounded by exceptionally smart peers who constantly challenged me. It felt as though I had transitioned from being a local champion to rubbing shoulders with truly brilliant individuals. I vividly remember my first day at this new school, beginning with a Chemistry class. Observing my new classmates and their impressive depth of understanding inspired me greatly. For the first time in years, I wasn't necessarily the smartest person in the room. It challenged my perspective profoundly and taught me an invaluable lesson: associating with people better than yourself pushes you to elevate your own game.

Thanks to my wit and charisma, I quickly made friends with almost everyone in the class, but my real focus was on the sharpest, most brilliant students. I wanted to get close enough to understand their techniques. Interestingly, I had recently rewatched 'Karate Kid,' recalling Sensei Mr. Miyagi advising his student to study the opponent's technique, emphasizing mastery as the path to honour and victory. In my case, though, these weren't opponents, but fellow students equally determined to excel academically and in life. My "intelligence mission" was to identify the most serious students, yet the playful, fun-loving side of my personality never left me. Striving to balance these two personas, I became known as someone smart yet approachable and enjoyable to be around. Although I never claimed the top spot in my class during my time at this school, I proudly remained among the best.

Some of the smartest students in my class were girls—young women whom I greatly admired and respected for their intelligence and dedication. Interestingly, one of these exceptional ladies had also won the same prestigious

Mathematics scholarship as I had, making us the two scholarship recipients in our class. The school maintained a special commendation list system, highlighting students who achieved a required number of distinctions in their subjects each term. This commendation list was essentially the school's Mount Rushmore, a prestigious acknowledgement of academic excellence. Whenever it was released, we all eagerly gathered to see who had made the cut and who hadn't. The anticipation intensified our motivation to study harder. Naturally, I made a personal vow never to miss being featured on this commendation list throughout my time at the school—a goal I proudly accomplished.

My new school provided many fond memories and valuable lessons. It was there I truly learned the importance of maximizing my free time. The top students in my class had a habit of studying diligently at every available opportunity, and I quickly adopted this practice. I began to appreciate how closely our habits—both positive and negative—are influenced by those we associate with. Additionally, I was appointed class captain, a role that affirmed my leadership abilities and demonstrated the trust my classmates and teachers placed in me. This responsibility was another testament to the reputation I had cultivated among peers and faculty alike.

As my secondary education drew to a close, I felt increasingly prepared to tackle the crucial examinations needed for university admission. The atmosphere around the school became intensely serious, as reality sank in for all of us—we were just one step away from fulfilling our dreams of becoming doctors, engineers, scientists, or pursuing other coveted careers we'd imagined. To support our goals, the school organized extra tutorials with a clear objective: excel in the exams on the first attempt, secure admission into top universities, and set our lives on the right path. However, lingering uncertainties overshadowed our excitement. We were acutely aware that achieving outstanding grades did not necessarily guarantee admission into our preferred programs. Many of us aspiring for prestigious professions understood the flawed university admission system, plagued by delays and overcrowding. Often, gaining admission to top federal universities required special connections, leaving merit-based applicants uncertain of their futures.

Fortunately, new opportunities began emerging around this time. Many reputable private universities had recently opened, offering parents who distrusted the unreliable public system and could afford the higher tuition a dependable alternative. Several classmates took advantage of this by simply completing their University Matriculation Exams and an additional entrance test. Almost overnight, many of them were already university freshmen. Additionally, those fortunate enough to hold dual citizenship or access international opportunities swiftly relocated, typically to universities in the United States or the United Kingdom. This was the dream for many of us, myself included, an aspiration I will explore further shortly. This was in the fall of 2002, immediately following our final term of high school. Meanwhile, others pursued alternative legitimate routes, such as pre-degree programs—a refined A-level scheme offered by some innovative public universities as a financial supplement and a lifeline for students for whom the traditional admission route had failed. I emphasize these details to highlight how significantly our self-esteem and confidence could suffer if we failed to enter university simultaneously with our peers. Nobody wanted to endure the awkwardness and demoralization of having nothing substantial to share when friends returned home during holidays and asked, "What are you up to these days?"

The Gathering Storm

With strong GCSE grades under my belt, I approached the University Matriculation exams with cautious optimism but not complete confidence. My first attempt was disastrous. Scoring below 200 out of 400, I experienced a profound blow to my self-esteem. That result was insufficient for any university admission. Deep down, I knew I hadn't given my best, yet accepting this was too painful. Instead, I quickly pivoted to Plan B: pursuing a university education in the United States. Without dual citizenship or financial means to afford full tuition, securing a scholarship became imperative.

I began intensive tutorials for the Scholastic Aptitude Test (SAT) and the Test of English as a Foreign Language (TOEFL). These tutorials brought me into a familiar circle—young dreamers aspiring to study abroad, each facing these two critical exams. For students like me, whose parents weren't particularly wealthy, the stakes felt especially high. Interestingly, these classes gathered students from various high schools across town, many sharing similar disappointments from their Matriculation exams.

When the time finally came, my SAT and TOEFL results weren't impressive enough for the scholarship offers I desperately needed. Within six months, I'd suffered a second crushing setback to my confidence. Still, I pressed on, quietly nursing my bruised pride. Encounters with former classmates already attending university intensified my sense of shame. I had once been among the best in my class, yet here I was, struggling just to gain admission.

Determined, I began submitting university applications, applying to no fewer than 20 institutions, some of which required application fees covered by my father. I nearly succeeded in obtaining a full-tuition scholarship from Berea College in Kentucky. My father had promised his full support if I received the scholarship, but in the final selection round, my application was rejected. At that moment, it felt as though my entire world had collapsed. In just nine months, my confidence took its third devastating hit, and this time, the blow was particularly severe. Local university admissions remained elusive, and the doors to foreign universities refused to open. This rejection pushed me to an all-time low. Every door seemed firmly closed, every pathway obscured. Desperate for a way to rebound, I searched relentlessly for new opportunities, but nothing appeared on the horizon. My dreams, once vivid and attainable, now seemed distant and unreachable, and the burden of uncertainty weighed heavily on me.

My father, seeing no other viable option, insisted I take the UME exams once more to secure admission into a Federal University. On this second attempt, I managed a modest improvement, scoring about 214 out of 400. However, this still wasn't enough to gain entry into a desirable program at my preferred university. This setback felt like a fourth punch to my gut, all within a single year. The academic excellence I had once proudly embodied now seemed like a distant memory, replaced by feelings of inadequacy and defeat.

The thought of staying home for another year was unbearable, especially when I considered my classmates who had already advanced well into their university journeys. By September 2004, I risked being two academic sessions behind my peers - and it was already mid-2003. During this challenging period, I often assisted my mother at her shop. This itself became a source of embarrassment since the shop was located just a short drive from my old high school, increasing my chances of running into former teachers or classmates. Each encounter heightened my sense of shame and inadequacy. Emotionally, academically, and psychologically, this was the lowest point I had ever reached. What compounded my struggle was the profound isolation; there was no one I felt comfortable talking to about my predicament. It felt as if everyone around me simply expected me to move on, even though I was stuck, painfully aware that my life should be progressing.

Reflecting on this period now, I realize the deep sense of failure I experienced wasn't uncommon among young people in Nigeria, many of whom faced significant difficulties gaining admission into their preferred universities. Though my struggle lasted just two years, it felt like an eternity to me at the time. However, once I finally secured university admission, I encountered peers whose journeys had been even more challenging—some having spent as long as ten years trying to gain entry. Their stories offered me perspective and humility, reshaping my understanding of perseverance and resilience.

Redemption

Around the end of June 2003, my dad called me with the suggestion I'd been dreading. "I think you should come with me to Lagos."

"Lagos? How?" I thought anxiously. Had things truly deteriorated so badly that living with my dad and stepmother was now the solution? I kept my expression neutral as he continued.

"You can try the University of Lagos Diploma programme," he proposed. "The entrance exam is next month, and this might still give you a chance to study your preferred course by September."

That was the only hopeful part of his suggestion, but it was overshadowed by my fear of moving to Lagos indefinitely. I was not ready to leave my comfort zone in as much as I began to regret not doing well at the University Matriculation Exams where I had chosen other Universities in the South West as my preferred option and not Lagos.

But for my father, practicality always took precedence. To him, it was straightforward: if he was to pay my fees and no other viable option existed, this was my best and possibly only chance to attend a reputable federal university that year. But also behind his decision was his desire to have me close enough to guide and mould me into a responsible adult. Looking back, it is clear to me now that God had a bigger plan, closing every other door except this one. It was through this singular path that my life's trajectory transformed significantly.

I recall the afternoon of our departure. My dad instructed me to pack that morning, but uncertainty lingered because my mother still opposed the move. Nonetheless, I packed, readying myself emotionally for what was next. As we prepared to leave, I opened the gates, and my dad drove the car out. He stopped briefly, looked at me, and asked bluntly, "Are you getting in or not?" Without hesitation, I placed my suitcase in the trunk, climbed into the car, and glanced back at the house, silently bidding it farewell. Little did I know that would be my last prolonged stay in that home, marking the beginning of an entirely new chapter in my life.

We arrived in Lagos, and my dad wasted no time in getting things started, instructing me immediately to obtain the form for the Diploma 2 program. This special entry program offered by the University of Lagos allowed students a trial year at the university. If they met the required Grade Point Average (GPA) for their chosen course, they progressed directly into the second year. It was an ideal scenario for me because I wouldn't lose any additional time. Although the program was costly, my dad, as always, was committed to investing in my education, believing firmly in my potential.

However, selecting my course of study became the source of my first major conflict with him. He strongly insisted on engineering, while I passionately rejected the idea. I preferred computer science, but after another heated discussion, I impulsively chose Estate Management—a program I had randomly spotted that seemed to align with my strongest subjects. To this day, I'm not entirely sure why I picked it; perhaps it was simply my way of asserting independence from my father's wishes. As the examination day rapidly approached, I poured myself into rigorous preparation. I knew this was an opportunity I couldn't afford to squander.

On the day of the exam, stepping into the crowded hall instantly brought back memories of my scholarship test—another intimidating sea of heads. Anxiety gripped me once more. I whispered a prayer and began the exam, quickly losing myself in answering the questions. When I finished, uncertainty lingered about my performance. A few weeks passed, and the results were finally released. We had to visit our respective faculties to check them. My anxiety soared; I dreaded facing a fifth disappointment within a single year.

When I arrived at the noticeboard, it was surrounded by a frantic crowd of students eager to find their names. I patiently waited for the commotion to subside before approaching. The names were listed from highest to lowest grades, with a cutoff of around 50%. Starting from the 90th position, I anxiously scanned upward, desperately seeking my name. Reaching second place without seeing it left me shattered. Fighting tears, I repeated the search to be sure but still found nothing. Dejected, I began walking away, already feeling defeated.

Then a sudden thought occurred to me that I hadn't checked who was number one. Turning back, I looked again. To my disbelief and joy, my name was at the very top, proudly occupying first place with a 90% score. My heart leapt with excitement, and I felt instantly vindicated after all my struggles. Bursting with joy, I hurried home to share the incredible news with my father. From that moment, the rest was history.

My Rebound Journey

My journey back to success through failure unfolded distinctly in six critical stages also depicted in the diagram below:

1. **Initial Success (Achievement)**: Early victories created confidence and self-belief.
2. **Complacency (Overconfidence)**: Overconfidence led to neglecting the practices and habits that created success.
3. **Setback (Failure):** Facing unexpected failures or humiliation due to complacency.

4. **Reflection (Awareness):** Honest introspection to identify the root cause of the failure

5. **Recommitment (Renewed Discipline):** Renewed dedication to habits and disciplines essential for success.

6. **Growth (Transformation):** Leveraging the lessons from failure to achieve new, sustainable levels of excellence.

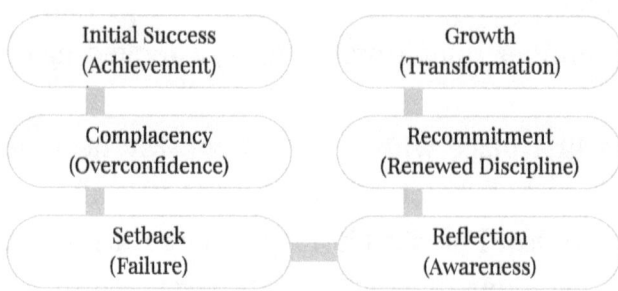

Figure 3.1 – The Rebound Journey

Initially, I experienced early success through winning the National Mathematics Scholarship, a triumph that boosted my confidence and self-belief tremendously. This early recognition validated my capabilities and set the stage for future victories.

However, with success came complacency. I gradually became overconfident, neglecting the very practices and disciplined routines—such as regular math practice—that had earned me initial success. This overconfidence eventually led me into a period of setbacks. An unexpectedly poor performance in an impromptu math test became a humbling and painful reminder of the consequences of my neglect. This later morphed into the frailties in other major exams that cost me crucial time.

This failure forced me into a period of deep reflection. I began to honestly introspect, identifying the root cause of my setback, and the abandonment of consistent, disciplined study habits. Not fully seizing the moments I had was also a factor. Realizing this truth marked a pivotal moment in my growth, guiding me toward renewed discipline.

With a clear awareness of my mistakes, I recommitted myself fully to the disciplined habits essential for success. I returned to rigorous study routines, restoring the diligence that had initially propelled my achievements. I took the last chance I had to get into University with unparalleled focus. This renewed discipline became the cornerstone of my recovery.

Finally, my journey culminated in significant personal growth and transformation. By leveraging the lessons learned from my failures, I established consistent and sustainable habits that not only restored my reputation and confidence but propelled me toward new, higher levels of excellence. The rebound journey taught me resilience, humility, and the critical importance of ongoing discipline, fundamentally reshaping my approach to life and success.

Reflections from the Valley

While I was deeply grateful to have found my way back to the top, the most profound insights that powered my growth came not during my victories, but from the valley of my lowest moments. We naturally detest failure and often fear it, but what if we viewed it differently? Even now in my chosen career as an academic, I have had to deal with rejections of my research in journals, which emphasized the fact that these lessons mean even more to me. I share five key insights I picked up along the way back to the top at my lowest moment:

1. **Failure is an event, not a person**: Throughout my experiences, especially when I struggled repeatedly to secure university admission, I realized that setbacks did not define who I was. Failing exams didn't make me a failure; they were merely moments—events—that eventually passed. Recognizing this allowed me to separate my identity from my circumstances and retain the confidence necessary to continue moving forward.

2. **Success is never-ending and failure is never final:** Each success or failure I experienced was temporary. Winning the scholarship felt wonderful, but it wasn't permanent. Likewise, my repeated admission failures felt crushing but were not the end. Understanding this dynamic gave me the courage to push beyond disappointment, knowing that as long as I persisted, neither success nor failure would mark the final chapter of my story.

3. **Treat success and failure as impostors:** Inspired by Rudyard Kipling's timeless poem "If," I learned the importance of meeting triumph and disaster with equal composure. The emotional highs of success and the lows of failure can both deceive us. My admission experiences taught me to stay balanced, neither becoming overly

confident when victorious nor excessively despondent in defeat.

4. **Failure is a powerful teacher:** My struggles profoundly taught me the value of persistence, humility, and resilience. The times I spent feeling embarrassed about my setbacks were moments of deep learning, helping me understand and empathize with others who faced even more challenging circumstances. These lessons became lifelong guides, reshaping my perspective on obstacles and growth.

5. **Failure clarifies purpose and direction:** Ironically, the course of study I randomly chose, Estate Management, became my unexpected pathway to renewed success. Initially picked out of defiance toward my father's wishes, this decision symbolized how failure and confusion can sometimes lead us toward clarity about our true interests and strengths. My journey affirmed that setbacks could be powerful guides, redirecting us toward the paths we are truly meant to follow.

Setbacks, when approached with reflection and renewed diligence, become catalysts for lasting triumph.

Wisdom Keys from Chapter 3

1. **Consistency Sustains Excellence** – Achievements are not just about talent or past victories; they require continuous discipline and effort. Letting go of the habits that brought success can quickly lead to setbacks.

2. **Humility is the Foundation of Growth** – Success can create a false sense of invincibility, but life has a way of humbling even the most accomplished. Staying teachable and disciplined is key to sustained success.

3. **Failure is a Pathway, Not a Destination** – Facing multiple failures in a short period can be disheartening, but perseverance through disappointment strengthens character and prepares you for bigger victories.

4. **Success has Unconventional Paths** – Sometimes, the road to your goals is not a straight line. Detours, delays, and unexpected opportunities—like the University of Lagos Diploma program—can still lead to success if you remain open to new possibilities.

Reflection Questions

1. Think of a time when overconfidence or neglect led to a setback in your life. How did you respond, and what lesson did you learn from the experience?

2. How have the people you surround yourself with influenced your growth—positively or negatively? What changes can you make to ensure your associations push you toward your goals?

3. Have you ever faced a moment where things didn't go as planned, but in hindsight, it turned out to be the best outcome? How can you trust the process even when things seem uncertain?

CHAPTER FOUR

Right People, Right Information, Right Time

"The right people with the right information at the right time can transform ordinary paths into extraordinary journeys."

– Adeyinka Adewale.

I concluded long ago that no individual truly achieves success alone. The notion of being entirely self-made simply doesn't hold up under scrutiny. We are, in fact, all products of countless contributions from people who have walked alongside us, whether briefly or throughout extended seasons. Sir Richard Branson, founder of The Virgin Group, wisely advised, "Surround yourself with people who bring out the best in you." His words underline the crucial role relationships play in shaping our journeys. History is rich with examples of widely celebrated individuals across all works of life whose success is traceable to having the right relationships.

Madam C.J. Walker, America's first Black female millionaire, who famously said, "Don't sit down and wait for the opportunities to come. Get up and make them" attributed her phenomenal success to the support of her network, mentors, and peers who helped her expand and distribute her revolutionary hair care products. George Washington Carver's groundbreaking agricultural innovations were not solely a result of his extraordinary intellect, but also deeply influenced by his relationships with professors and mentors at Tuskegee Institute, notably Booker T. Washington. Similarly, Robert F. Smith, one of America's wealthiest Black entrepreneurs, attributes his success significantly to the mentorship and guidance he received throughout his finance career, connecting him with pivotal networks and opportunities. Oprah Winfrey, one of the world's most influential media personalities, similarly credits her phenomenal success to the wisdom and mentorship of Maya Angelou, whose guidance shaped Oprah's thinking during critical career moments. Their stories exemplify the powerful truth that connections can redefine our possibilities.

This reality became profoundly clear in my own journey. Every significant milestone I reached, be it in academics, business, or personal growth, was deeply influenced by individuals I encountered along the way. Professors who saw my potential long before I recognized it, friends who urged me beyond my comfort zone, and mentors who provided invaluable guidance, all formed the invisible force driving my progress. The people we surround ourselves with profoundly impact our vision, expand our opportunities, and dramatically accelerate our success. In university, I experienced firsthand how meaningful connections do more than simply open doors - they transform life's trajectory itself.

RPIT Model

Reflecting on my life's journey, I've traced nearly every significant milestone back to this simple yet powerful principle – Right people, Right information, Right time. When you are surrounded by the right people, the right information gets to you at the right time. Conversely, being surrounded by the wrong people tends to produce the opposite effect. Imagine it as a finely tuned mesh-and-gear mechanism: the most crucial gear, the largest driving component of the entire system, is having the right people in your circle. Their influence sets the entire process in motion, shaping your trajectory and amplifying your potential.

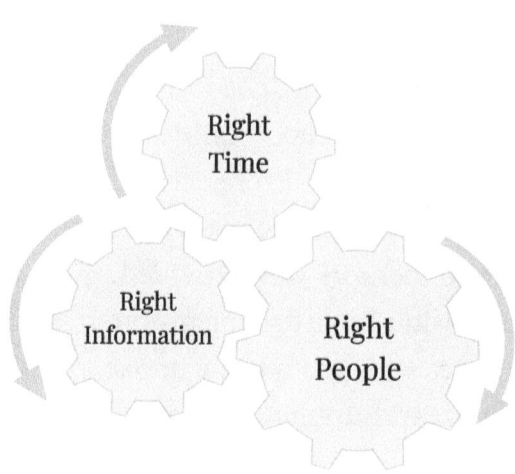

Figure 4.1 – RPIT Model

At the University of Lagos, I found myself in circles that challenged me, sharpened my thinking, and pushed me toward excellence. I met mentors who saw what I could become and encouraged me to pursue greater opportunities. I formed friendships that fuelled my ambition, providing the support I needed to navigate challenges. Every conversation, every piece of advice, and every opportunity extended to me was a reminder that relationships are not just social connections, they are bridges to a greater future. I saw how words are so powerful that they can either build us up or tear us down. The words of the people we surround ourselves with shape our beliefs, influence our decisions and ultimately determine the direction of our lives. A mentor's encouragement can spark confidence, a friend's advice can provide clarity, and a single conversation can ignite a life-changing idea. When we are constantly exposed to voices that challenge us to grow, remind us of our potential, and push us toward excellence, we begin to see ourselves through a lens of possibility rather than limitation. As Henry Ford famously said, "Whether you think you can, or you think you can't—you're right." The words we hear and internalize from our mentors and positive associations become the foundation upon which our success is built. If there is one lesson to take away, it is this: Choose your circle wisely, because the right relationships will take you places you never imagined possible.

At different stages of my life, I've come to deeply appreciate the people God strategically placed along my journey as guiding voices during pivotal seasons. One memorable afternoon in my second year at university, I encountered such a voice, a lecturer from my department whose commanding presence and authoritative tone instantly captivated me. Tall, fair, and somewhat imposing, he spoke with audacious confidence that initially seemed to border on pride. Yet, beneath his intimidating exterior lay a wisdom and clarity I found irresistible. His words carried a prophetic weight, resonating deeply with me, particularly in how precisely he linked our youthful decisions to our future outcomes. Apart from my father, whose mentorship had consistently guided me, this was the first time I was opening myself up to other voices with such profound influence. Professor Nubi taught Town Planning exclusively to final-year students, meaning I had three years before officially becoming his student. But waiting that long felt impossible, given the wisdom he freely shared.

Driven by curiosity and perhaps desperation, I made a bold choice. Every Friday at 8 AM, I attended his lectures, even though I wasn't yet in his class. Unable to enter the lecture hall, I sat on the floor outside, taking meticulous notes. Although his subject was Town Planning, he consistently dedicated the first half-hour to sharing practical life lessons, which proved incredibly therapeutic for me.

It was during one such session that I first heard of Ben Carson and his remarkable book, "Gifted Hands." Profoundly inspired, I promptly read every available work by Carson. Among Professor Nubi's invaluable lessons was the importance of staying grounded and choosing wisdom over popularity or shortcuts. He often reminded students that time inevitably distinguishes the wise from the foolish. At every class reunion, he said, the long-term outcomes of our choices would be unmistakably clear - and he was right. Looking back, though his words sometimes seemed harsh and his future outlook stern, I realized the depth and power of the wisdom he imparted. His counsel weren't widely popular among students, yet he commanded respect and even fear because we could perceive his insights were profound, and transformative.

Around the same time, there was a noticeable rise of motivational speakers across the country - dynamic men and women gifted with the profound ability to articulate life's purpose and stir deep inspiration. Figures like Fela Durotoye spoke words that profoundly shifted my mindset and transformed my life. Niyi Adesanya, with his powerful teachings on leadership, spurred me to shift the gears of my journey. I eagerly attended any campus event featuring these speakers, consistently amazed by their insightful wisdom and their talent for breathing life into weary hearts. Acquiring their message recordings on CDs felt like discovering hidden treasure.

Among these influential voices was Rev. Dr. Sam Adeyemi, whose Excellence in Leadership conferences introduced transformative perspectives on navigating changing times. These remarkable individuals expanded my vision, permitting me to dream far beyond my immediate circumstances. Their words challenged me to cast bold visions, write them down, and passionately pursue them. Reflecting now, I share this with immense gratitude, knowing that their teachings significantly influenced many of the meaningful pursuits I undertook during my university years. Everyone needs voices that speak directly to their potential and greatness, and these speakers served precisely that role in my life. They may not know me personally, but their impact on my journey remains unforgettable. God undeniably used their voices to shape and clarify my purpose, laying the foundations for my life's path.

During this period, as part of an initiative celebrating scholars, the University invited Mrs. Ibukun Awosika to speak at the Multipurpose Hall of the University of Lagos. To a packed auditorium, Mrs. Awosika recounted her remarkable journey—from graduating with a third-class degree from one of Nigeria's top universities to founding one of the country's most successful furniture enterprises. Her audacity and determination left me utterly inspired. Her eloquence and grace deeply resonated with me, revealing new possibilities through her life and further illuminating the significance of the many voices God was placing in my path. I often describe this phase as my season of inspiration. Everywhere I turned, it seemed God had strategically positioned someone whose voice spoke directly to my potential. These positive role models served as voices of truth, guiding me toward greatness. In these moments, I felt God's presence clearly, speaking powerfully through them.

On a more practical level, I also recognized how God carefully placed individuals in my life for specific purposes. He addressed my academic, professional, and spiritual growth through various mentors who became essential voices during critical stages. Inspiration consistently led to growth. My first professional mentor, Mr. John Zedomi of John Zedomi and Associates, gave me my initial exposure to corporate life outside my father's surveying practice. Introduced through a senior colleague, Mr. Zedomi became instrumental in my development. His office became my refuge from personal difficulties at home. Mr. Zedomi patiently listened, encouraged me, and provided numerous opportunities for professional growth. His faith in my abilities pushed me toward greater excellence; he involved me in high-level meetings and invested in management training, introducing me to influential books like "Seven Habits of Highly Effective People" and "Eat That Frog." It was also through his training initiatives that I learned about Jack Welch, the legendary CEO of General Electric, whose management insights further solidified my leadership foundation.

Some of my professors became trusted advisors and significant influencers in my life. Professor Austin Otegbulu was one such mentor, generously sharing his knowledge and offering guidance that impacted both my academic and professional pursuits. He later invited me to work at his firm in Abuja, facilitating my early major publications and mentoring me in specialized aspects of real estate, particularly Professional and Business Ethics. His mentorship profoundly shaped my master's dissertation and subsequent PhD in this field. Professor Omirin, another influential figure, epitomized grace, humility, and brilliance, inspiring me academically and spiritually. Her admirable character and intellectual strength motivated me deeply; she became a maternal figure to many students, myself included. Her status as an alumnus led me to choose the University of Reading for my postgraduate studies. When I graduated, she gifted me a Bible, inscribed with a powerful message: "Let your light so shine that they may see your good works and glorify your Father in heaven." Those words continue to guide me today. Additionally, I benefited from the mentorship of peers, and exceptional colleagues, who generously provided practical academic support, significantly enhancing my preparation and performance.

On a spiritual level, God also brought dedicated individuals whose focused walk with Him greatly inspired me. During a critical period of rekindling my spiritual journey, these relationships offered my first authentic experiences of discipleship, setting the stage for an even deeper spiritual transformation during my year of national service in Abuja—a time marked by profound spiritual growth, preparing me for the next significant phase of my life.

Passing the Leadership Test

In my final year at university, I had the rare privilege of leading the Christian fellowship in my faculty, the Faculty of Environmental Sciences Students' Fellowship (FESSF). It was my first significant experience guiding others spiritually, placing me at the forefront of a responsibility I'd never previously imagined. This role sparked within me an even greater vision for impacting a large group of young people. Committed to this new assignment, I deepened my prayer life and regularly shared insights from God's word every Friday.

During one of my quiet times, I felt strongly inspired to organise a program intended to bless five hundred students on campus. It was an ambitious goal, motivated by the influential voices of my mentors. I drafted a plan and reached out to a few friends for support, but they weren't interested or couldn't see the vision. Whilst my search continued, I learned that a friend had become president of another larger student fellowship affiliated with a prominent church. I shared my vision with him, and he immediately agreed to help secure the high-profile speakers I wanted, although I had to finance the event myself. I prepared a detailed proposal and sought sponsorship from different banks without success. However, a conversation with my first boss about my initiative provided an unexpected opportunity. He referred me to his friend at a financial services firm. I eagerly seized this chance, submitted my proposal, and was invited to present to their board. My presentation impressed the board, and they agreed to sponsor me with 300,000 Naira, but only after confirming the event's success by attending themselves.

This condition presented a challenge. I had no upfront funds. With unpaid vendors and a booked but unpaid venue costing 120,000 Naira, anxiety gripped me. I prayed fervently for divine intervention, and it arrived dramatically. Just a day before the event, overwhelmed and desperate, I visited another mentor, explaining my situation. Compassionately, she wrote me a cheque for 80,000 Naira, her entire salary for that month, trusting I would repay after the event. Deeply moved, I quickly cashed the cheque, paying vendors, but was still short of funds for the venue. On event day at 7 am, the decorator called to inform me he'd found the hall already open and asked if he could begin work. I nervously agreed, praying no issues would arise.

By evening, the hall was filled and the event was a resounding success, and my sponsors were thoroughly impressed. True to their word, they handed me the promised 300,000 Naira cheque.

This event proved once again the incredible power of having the right people around. I cleared all debts, repaid my mentor, and had 60,000 Naira left, which I intended to reward myself with. Yet, as I stepped outside to reflect, God spoke clearly: "You won't touch that money. You will give it all away." Stunned and resistant, I knew better than to disobey. I immediately understood the purpose, to provide scholarships for ten brilliant but indigent students in my faculty, each receiving 6,000 Naira. That obedience, I believe, paved the way for the £100,000 PhD scholarship I later received from the University of Reading. I also believe God was testing where my heart was – with the people under my care or with material possessions. I chose the former.

At the heart of every significant achievement lies a fundamental truth: no one succeeds alone. Our dreams, accomplishments, and impact are shaped by the relationships we cultivate, the knowledge we gain, and the pivotal moments that define our journeys. Reflecting again on my RPIT model (Right People, Right Information, Right Time), I've realized how profoundly a single mentor can guide us, how a supportive network can open doors, and how timely conversations can redirect our paths entirely. Every milestone I've reached underscores the importance of collaboration in accelerating success. Building strong relationships and pursuing meaningful partnerships isn't optional, it's essential. Those we surround ourselves with either propel or hinder our progress; they feed our vision or limit our potential. Intentionally cultivating relationships with inspiring, challenging, and supportive individuals positions us for exponential growth.

Reflecting on my journey, one powerful lesson remains clear: great dreams are rarely realized alone. The larger the vision, the stronger the relationships required to bring it to life. Truly, no person is an island. Success is a collective effort, and building greatness requires building together.

Five Essential Relationships

My reflections above captured five types of people or relationships whose roles were invaluable in accelerating my personal growth and success:

1. **Mentors:** Mentors are seasoned guides who share their wisdom, experiences, and insights to help us navigate our paths more effectively. They offer advice, encouragement, and direction, often illuminating opportunities and pitfalls we might otherwise overlook.

2. **Coaches:** Coaches are skilled in drawing out our best performance. They provide structured feedback, clear guidance, and accountability, helping us refine our skills and achieve specific goals. Coaches bring a disciplined approach, ensuring we stay committed and focused.

3. **Pastors or Spiritual Leaders:** Pastors or spiritual leaders nurture our spiritual well-being, offering counsel and wisdom that helps us maintain emotional balance and moral clarity. They provide comfort, hope, and perspective during challenging times, grounding us with principles and values.

4. **Peers (Friends and Colleagues):** Peers serve as companions who journey alongside us, offering support, encouragement, and camaraderie. They can challenge us intellectually, push us beyond our comfort zones, and offer invaluable perspectives shaped by shared experiences.

5. **Connectors:** Connectors specialize in creating opportunities by introducing us to the right networks. Their strength lies in their vast connections, bringing us valuable information, contacts, and resources exactly when we need them, thus accelerating our growth and success.

	Primary Role	**Value Added**	**Information Provided**
Mentor	Guidance & Wisdom	Long-term vision and strategic advice	Insights, personal experiences, life lessons
Coach	Performance & Accountability	Discipline, motivation, goal-setting	Structured feedback, skill-building, action plans
Pastor/ Spiritual Leader	Spiritual & Emotional Support	Moral clarity, emotional balance	Encouragement, spiritual teachings, counsel
Peers (Friends/ Colleagues)	Support & Challenge	Emotional support, healthy competition	Diverse perspectives, shared experiences
Connectors	Networking & Opportunities	Access to new possibilities	Valuable contacts, timely resources, opportunities

Table 4.1 – The Types of People Necessary for Personal Growth and Success

Having these essential types of individuals in your life ensures you receive the right guidance, support, and opportunities needed for meaningful growth and sustained success. Even though I could see God's hands in positioning the right people around me, my response to them was even more crucial. That was what unlocked the opportunities that they had for me.

Wisdom Keys from Chapter 4

1. **Your Circle Is Your Catalyst:** Who you surround yourself with determines the trajectory of your life. Mentors, friends, and associates can either elevate your potential or hinder your growth. Choose your circle wisely.

2. **Proximity to Greatness Inspires Greatness:** Being in the presence of visionary thinkers, mentors, and positive role models ignites ambition and expands your perspective. Seeking out and learning from accomplished individuals accelerates personal and professional growth.

3. **Giving Opens the Doors to Greater Blessings:** True success is not just about personal achievement but also about impacting others. The act of selfless giving, as seen in providing scholarships, often unlocks unexpected rewards and divine favour.

4. **The Right Voices Reveal the Right Opportunities:** Sometimes, all it takes is one conversation, one lecture, or one book recommendation to shift your path. When you're surrounded by wise voices, you see doors you didn't know existed.

Reflection Questions

1. Who are the people currently shaping your life, and how are they influencing your mindset, decisions, and aspirations?

2. Think of a time when someone's words or actions changed your trajectory. How can you intentionally seek more relationships that inspire and challenge you?

3. How have you used your success to uplift others? What steps can you take to be a source of mentorship, guidance, or support for someone else?

CHAPTER FIVE

Carpe Diem! Seize the Moment!

"As long as it is day, we must do the works of him who sent me. Night is coming when no one can work."

– *Jesus Christ.*

The old man sat on a park bench, tossing breadcrumbs to the pigeons. A young businessman, glued to his phone, nearly tripped over the elder's outstretched cane.

"In a hurry?" the old man chuckled.

"Always," the young man replied, barely glancing up.

The elder smiled. "Funny thing about life, you rush through it, and one day you realize you were running past all the good parts."

He reached into his pocket and pulled out a yellowed napkin with a quote scribbled in shaky handwriting:

"Dum loquimur, fugerit invida aetas: carpe diem, quam minimum credula postero." ("While we speak, envious time will have fled: seize the day, trusting as little as possible in the future.")

The young man read it and frowned. "Horace?"

The old man nodded. "And yet, people still need reminding."

Like the young businessman, we all need to be reminded often of the need to slow down and take in the moments we have. This is what Carpe Diem is about, embracing life while it's happening. No matter how fast we run, time always runs faster. And unlike pigeons, lost moments never come back for breadcrumbs. A wise man once said to me that many people pass through the university but never let the university pass through them. I thought it was one of the usual cliches until I found myself in the four walls of the University of Lagos.

Lagos is a city that moves at lightning speed; blink, and you might miss your chance. Everything around me seemed to race at a thousand miles per hour. Classes followed one another rapidly, chasing lecturers became a routine, and even grabbing lunch meant rushing to avoid the endless queues. Life was relentlessly fast-paced. Yet amid the chaos, there were defining moments that transformed my life. These opportunities appear swiftly and can be easily missed if one isn't attentive. Thankfully, by God's grace, I managed to seize them, profoundly altering my life's trajectory.

You might have heard the saying, "Chance is what happens when preparation meets opportunity." Upon entering the university, I understood the stakes were high, prompting me to consistently give my best effort. The Diploma program allowed me to take foundational courses over two semesters, after which my average GPA would determine my advancement to Year 2.

Having chosen the five-year Estate Management programme, I excelled significantly during my Diploma year, achieving an impressive 4.67 CGPA out of 5, well above the required 2.5 needed for progression. This stellar performance not only ensured my smooth transition to Year 2 but also earned me the role of class representative once again.

Integrating into the new class, composed of students who entered through the regular University Matriculation Exams pathway, I quickly formed remarkable friendships and encountered some fascinating individuals. My academic excellence continued, highlighted by a GPA of 4.88 in the first semester of my second year, comprising all distinctions and a single B. By the end of the second semester, my cumulative GPA stood at 4.79.

This period coincided with the University of Lagos introducing an Honours Students system, rewarding students with CGPAs of 4.5 and above. Benefits included annual cash awards, priority access to free accommodation—which my father declined since we lived near the campus—and other privileges. Yet, the most impactful, though less publicised, benefit was being included in a select group of scholars called upon for "special duties." Two such special duties profoundly impacted my journey. I'd share one in this chapter.

The Case Competition That Transformed My University Experience

During my time at the university, I built an excellent relationship with our Head Counsellor, Mrs. Asiwaju. She had become like a mother figure to me and many other scholars. Often, I'd visit her office simply to check in and see if there was anything new she needed us to do—a special yet unwritten privilege of being an honours student.

One afternoon, my department's secretary called me to pick up a letter. Curious and pleasantly surprised, I hurried over. I'll never forget the title on that envelope: "Invitation to Participate in a Global Case Study Competition." The aim was to select four individuals from Nigeria who would represent the country and the entire African continent in Budapest, Hungary.

Initially, I was uncertain whether this was meant for me, but my name appeared on the letter, neatly printed on KPMG letterhead. Here's a confession: at that time, I had no idea what KPMG was—I mistakenly thought it was a plastic manufacturing company! Nor did I know what a "case study competition" entailed. Given that internet access was hourly charged at cybercafés back then, I quickly spent a few hours researching. Soon, I discovered that KPMG was one of the leading accounting firms globally, part of the "Big Four." I also familiarized myself with case studies and their methodology.

With two weeks until the selection aptitude test, I diligently refreshed my maths and comprehension skills, reminiscent of my previous preparations for my unsuccessful attempt at studying in the United States. On test day, knowing I'd be entering a professional environment, I dressed impeccably: a light blue shirt, dark blue tie, black jacket, and grey trousers, a Primark suit my father had purchased during one of his UK visits. Upon arriving at the KPMG office, I was surprised to find that 19 other students from my university had also been invited; only two of us were from Environmental Sciences. While many appeared casual, even unkempt, at first, I felt overdressed and out of place. Once the test began, my discomfort grew as some participants swiftly completed their exams while I struggled, feeling increasingly rusty.

Just as panic began to set in, a young woman entered the room confidently, smiling warmly. To my surprise, she bypassed everyone else, came directly to me, and asked, "What's your name?" After I answered, she quietly left. To this day, I'm unsure why she singled me out, but something tells me my professional appearance made the difference. The lesson became clear: always show up prepared, present yourself with excellence, and be ready for your moment.

After completing the test, we faced an anxious 72-hour wait for the results. Given the competition, I wasn't optimistic. Yet, to my astonishment, another letter arrived days later, congratulating me for passing the test round and inviting me to an assessment centre, where the final four would be chosen. The initial round had reduced the pool by half, leaving only ten of us. Despite my lingering doubts, I advanced once more, realizing yet again the remarkable power of preparation and presence.

It was in this round that I felt truly thrown into the deep end. What exactly was an assessment centre? What would it involve? I hurriedly went to a cyber cafe to seek answers online, discovering it would include various group exercises designed to evaluate our critical thinking, analytical abilities, and teamwork skills. With limited knowledge, I prepared as best as I could. On the day of the assessment, maintaining my corporate attire, I stepped into the conference room unsure of what awaited me. Yet, even the little preparation I'd done proved invaluable.

We were divided into two groups of five, each assigned a business scenario to solve. Each participant received specific insights and data related to their assigned role within a hypothetical company's management issue. I was appointed the Sales and Marketing executive. However, the challenge was that we had to collaborate effectively, voluntarily sharing our distinct information to collectively solve the broader problem under strict time constraints.

Immediately, a gentleman in my group took charge but quickly made two crucial mistakes. First, he attempted to read another team member's information card, which was against the rules. Second, he overlooked a young woman in our group who appeared overwhelmed, launching directly into solution mode without including her input. Recognizing the oversight, I politely intervened, inviting the young lady to share her perspective with the group. This simple action earned me crucial points, teaching me an invaluable leadership lesson: true influence often lies not in dominance or noise but in quiet, thoughtful actions.

Advancing to the final six candidates, from whom the final four representing Nigeria and Africa in Budapest, Hungary, would be chosen, we moved immediately into the final phase. I was uncertain about what lay ahead. When summoned to a separate room, I noticed a thick, 30-page document labelled "Harvard Business Case Study," alongside another sheet outlining the questions we needed to address. Fear instantly gripped me. Business studies had been a sore point since high school, where poor teaching had fostered a lasting aversion. My avoidance of business-related subjects had steered me toward the sciences instead. Now, completely alone, I faced an overwhelming task: analyse comprehensive business data and develop solutions without any prior expertise.

Yet, I pressed forward. Sometimes, life's preparation for greatness occurs subtly and imperceptibly. Little did I know, that experiences like helping my mother with her roadside business, learning plumbing from my father, staff training during my initial internship, working in my father's modest office, and negotiating prices at local markets would blend seamlessly into a powerful foundation, equipping me to address complex corporate challenges from a Harvard Business School case study.

Nervously, I began jotting down my ideas on the flip chart, quickly performing numerical analyses - after all, I had been a maths scholar. To my relief, creative ideas began to flow, and before I knew it, my solutions took shape. Soon after, I was ushered into a larger boardroom where my flip chart was prominently displayed for a panel of senior partners from the firm. As I began presenting, to my astonishment, they erupted in applause. It was completely unexpected. Being the first to present that day, I'd made a powerful impression. The pride, elation, and gratitude I felt at that moment were indescribable. It was a pivotal turning point that profoundly shaped my self-belief and future ambitions. My confidence surged, reinforcing the belief, "I can achieve anything if I truly set my mind to it." Every experience counts, none is wasted.

Amid these uplifting reflections, I received the incredible news: not only had I made the final team, but I'd also been appointed the team captain. The excitement was overwhelming. Unfortunately, this joy was short-lived, as just weeks later, our trip to Budapest was abruptly cancelled. Our visa applications had been submitted too late, and the Hungarian Embassy couldn't process them in time. The disappointment was crushing; I'd eagerly anticipated my first international trip, representing Africa on the global stage.

Despite the setback, God's intricate ways soon became evident. During that period, I connected with remarkable individuals, some of whom remain lifelong friends. More importantly, looking back, I see clearly that God had been giving me a glimpse into my future. Unbeknownst to me, those events marked my subtle yet definite shift into the world of business and management—a field I'd previously disliked and actively avoided. Today, as a Professor in this very field, I'm continually amazed at how God uses unexpected experiences to shape and guide us toward our destiny.

Just as Horace warned the hurried young man about missed opportunities, my KPMG experience sparked in me the realization that the university had far more to offer than simply earning a degree. In seizing an unlikely opportunity, I discovered untapped potential within myself. Gradually, my university journey became less about academic achievement alone and more about developing a voice and perspective God would use globally.

Opportunities constantly surround us. Recognizing them is one challenge; taking advantage of them is another. Academic excellence had positioned me perfectly to encounter extraordinary opportunities—and I chose to embrace each one. Even when uncertain of outcomes or lacking confidence, I consistently permitted myself to try, framing my efforts by simply asking: "What could I lose by trying?" Remarkably, every single attempt enriched my growth in immeasurable ways.

Recognising and Harnessing Opportunities

Looking back on my case competition experience and beyond, I've come to realise that many of the most transformative moments in my life came disguised as ordinary or even inconvenient situations. Whether it was the surprise of being invited to a global case study competition I didn't fully understand, or standing alone in a room with a daunting Harvard Business School case study and nothing but a flipchart and my wits, every defining moment was born out of my willingness to say yes - to try, to show up, and to grow.

When I think about how far I've come, it's clear to me now that preparation truly meets opportunity in the most unexpected ways. Every skill I had picked up—from helping my mother with her roadside business to listening attentively in management training sessions, to simply observing the world around me formed a reservoir I could draw from in those moments that mattered most.

One of the clearest parallels I've found is in the story of William Kamkwamba, known as "The Boy Who Harnessed the Wind." Growing up in rural Malawi, William faced poverty and famine. With limited formal education, he taught himself how to build a windmill from scrap materials to bring electricity to his village. Like me, he didn't start with everything he needed—but he was prepared in heart and mindset. His story resonates deeply with mine: the courage to act despite not knowing everything, the willingness to learn, and the power of showing up fully when the moment arrived.

In both our stories, one thing is clear: no moment is ever wasted if you approach it with the right mindset.

Key Mindsets to Seize Your Moment:

- **Growth Mindset:** Be willing to learn, adapt, and improve, even when the task seems overwhelming.

- **Optimism:** Believe that something good can come from trying, even when others don't see it.

- **Determination:** Keep going, even when the path is uncertain.

- **Proactivity:** Don't wait for the perfect moment—step forward and meet it.

- **Humility:** Remain teachable, knowing that each experience, person, or setback might be preparing you for something greater.

Ultimately, seizing opportunities is not about having all the answers but about having the posture to learn, the heart to try, and the courage to move forward—even when the outcome is uncertain. My story and William's are proof that the right mindset can turn even the most ordinary moments into life-changing breakthroughs.

Wisdom Keys from Chapter 5

1. **Opportunities Often Come Disguised as Challenges** – Life-changing moments don't always appear as grand invitations. Sometimes, they come in the form of unexpected tests, intimidating challenges, or moments of uncertainty. Recognizing these disguised opportunities is key to unlocking success.

2. **Courage to Try Is the First Step to Success:** Fear of failure stops many from seizing life-changing opportunities. The willingness to step out, even when uncertain of the outcome, often leads to incredible growth, unexpected victories, and new paths you never imagined.

3. **Failure to Act often births Regret:** In the long run, we often regret the chances we didn't take more than the mistakes we made. Even when things don't go as planned, taking action always leads to growth, experience, and new doors opening.

4. **Every Experience Contributes to Your Future:** No moment in life is wasted. Even seemingly insignificant experiences—helping in a family business, past failures, or minor academic struggles—often prepare you for success in ways you don't realize until much later.

Reflection Questions

1. Think about a time when hesitation or fear stopped you from pursuing something. How would your life be different if you had seized that moment?

2. Are you open to the possibility that your path may unfold differently than you planned? How can you embrace unexpected turns as part of a greater purpose?

3. What skills, lessons, or past experiences do you have that might be preparing you for an opportunity you haven't yet recognized? How can you leverage them?

CHAPTER SIX

More Wins, More Possibilities

"Success breeds confidence, and confidence breeds more opportunities."

- Jack Welch, former CEO of General Electric.

Success is a springboard, not a finish line. Those who adopt a growth mindset understand that every achievement expands their capacity to achieve even more. With each win, the mind stretches, confidence grows, and new possibilities emerge. It is this mindset, the belief that success builds upon itself, that transforms ordinary people into extraordinary achievers.

When Sara Blakely, the founder of Spanx first launched her shapewear brand, she had no background in fashion, no investors, and no business degree - just a great idea and relentless determination. When her first product gained traction, she didn't stop to celebrate for long; instead, she asked herself, "What else can I create? How far can I take this?" That curiosity and belief in possibilities led her to expand Spanx into a billion-dollar empire. Her initial success was not the end, it was the doorway to even bigger dreams. Similarly, many of the most celebrated individuals in the world of business today leveraged every breakthrough they had as the confidence to think bigger. That is the power of a mindset that embraces possibilities. The more you achieve, the more you realize what is possible. A mind that has grown to embrace possibilities does not settle. It asks, *"What's next?" and "How far can I go?"*

After the case competition experience, something ignited within me—an inner fire that propelled me toward even greater accomplishments. When we come to understand that each win is not just a victory, but evidence of our potential, we begin to unlock a world of limitless opportunities. Success, I've learned, isn't about reaching a final destination. It's about realising that there are no ceilings. That mindset shift would go on to define my experience at the University of Lagos.

In the academic year following the competition, my confidence soared. I began setting bold academic goals, the most significant of which was this: I resolved to remain a straight-A student for the rest of my time at the university. I didn't take that decision lightly. After writing it down, I knelt in prayer, committing the goal to God. At that point, my faith was also deepening. I had come to see clearly that nothing I'd experienced up to that point had been by chance—God's hand had been guiding me all along.

One scripture stood out to me, and I held onto it tightly: Proverbs 3:5—"Trust in the Lord with all your heart, and lean not on your understanding; in all your ways acknowledge Him, and He will direct your path." I knew I couldn't rely solely on my intellect or ability. I had to trust Him completely. Around that same period, I did something I had never done before. As an act of faith, I gave what I considered a sacrificial offering—a seed. It was just five hundred Naira, the equivalent of about 25 pence in today's exchange rate, but back then, it was my entire weekly allowance. It wasn't about the amount; it was about the heart behind it. That act of surrender was my way of saying, "God, I trust You to show up."

What happened next would blow my mind. It reaffirmed a truth I've since come to live by: spiritual laws and indeed principles are no respecter of persons. Anyone who acts in alignment with those laws will receive the results they promise. That season marked the beginning of a powerful transformation, both spiritually and academically.

How I became an accidental entrepreneur at the University

An academic year after my transformative experience with KPMG, I found myself becoming an accidental entrepreneur. Looking back, I know I would never have seen—let alone seized—the opportunity if not for the confidence and mindset shift that occurred the year before.

It all started casually. A few friends were discussing an assignment that was due the next day. They sounded confused and unmotivated to tackle the task. I was eavesdropping at first, but before I knew it, I walked over and said, "Let me do your assignment for you—for a fee."

They were stunned. Frankly, so was I.

"How much?" one of them asked.

"1,500 Naira," I replied.

At the time, the exchange rate was about 250 Naira to a British pound, so my charge was less than £10. In my mind, I figured there was no way he'd accept. But with a brief pause, he said, "Deal. Let's do it."

His friend immediately chimed in: "Me too."

Just like that, I had made 3,000 Naira, six times what I had sacrificially given to God the month before, and six times my weekly allowance. I asked them to pay 50% upfront, and they did. For the first time in my university life, I had real cash in hand—proper cash! I rushed to a business centre, bought packs of floppy disks, paid for computer time at the cybercafé, and began researching. That night, fuelled by adrenaline and excitement, I pulled an all-nighter. I crafted polished assignments with sleek covers and delivered both projects the following day.

They were thrilled, not just with the quality, but with the speed. They paid the remaining balance without hesitation and immediately began spreading the word. More students came my way. The business started booming. At one point, I was making so much money I'd forget to collect my weekly allowance from my dad. I began using my earnings to invest in books - books that would go on to shape my thinking and fuel my growth. One profound lesson emerged in that season: excellence always wins. Wherever it shows up, it opens doors.

As demand increased, I found myself working on more than ten assignments for the same module—one I was enrolled in myself. To avoid plagiarism, I began innovating, creating uniquely written and styled submissions for each client. It pushed me into new realms of creativity and originality. Importantly, I never cut corners. I delivered high-quality work and gave each client value for their money. As the business grew, I raised my prices—not just to match the demand, but to filter out those who weren't serious. In just nine months, I saw a threefold increase in my earnings. The initial 3,000 Naira deal evolved into projects where I earned 10,000 Naira.

Soon, affluent students began seeking my services. Some paid generously, while others took me out to restaurants I previously couldn't afford. They introduced me to more influential peers, expanding not only my client base but also my network. My network expanded. My purse expanded. My mind expanded. I was living a new kind of life and it all began with a single moment of boldness, backed by preparation and the pursuit of excellence.

The Entrepreneurship Mindset

This was when I truly learned that entrepreneurship is, at its core, a mindset. On the mountain of entrepreneurship, it's not just the truth that sets you free—it's the truth you act upon. Action is the key. Inspired by this realisation, I began diversifying my ventures. One of my short-term wins was selling water at school parties, and to my surprise, I made a substantial profit. But I wasn't doing any of this alone. I built a network—a team of partners who each brought something valuable to the table.

One friend allowed me to use his room as my workspace. A few of my lecturers, seeing my drive, gave me access to their wealth of wisdom and internet facility. A local food vendor near my faculty lent me cooling containers whenever I needed them for my water-selling gigs. Another partner provided his car to help me shop for supplies. The list of collaborators was endless.

I didn't operate in isolation. I built partnerships. I formed teams. I refused to see anyone as a competition. Instead, I viewed every individual as a potential collaborator, people with whom I could work and create value. This approach granted me access to resources I didn't always possess but frequently needed to execute my plans effectively.

In essence, with the right partners comes access to the right resources and the ability to carry out key activities that move your business or idea forward. The operative word here is "key." While many people can be potential partners, only a select few are strategically positioned to provide exactly what you need when you need it. Identifying and working with those key individuals is what drives success. Entrepreneurship, I learned, is less about doing everything yourself and more about unlocking the right doors with the right keys—people, resources, and action.

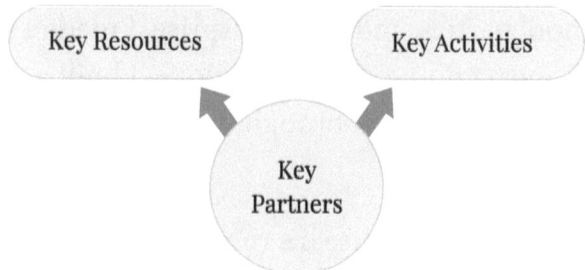

Figure 6.1 – The Power of Key Partners

Both of my businesses began to flourish, though I eventually shut down the water venture after a few successful runs. While it was highly profitable, I realised the operational demands weren't sustainable in the long term. Looking back, it was a wise decision. Knowing when to continue or quit a business can save you unnecessary stress and preserve your energy for what truly matters.

With that clarity, I scaled up my assignment business, eventually expanding into writing full dissertations. These projects were more demanding, but they came with significantly higher pay. I began charging tens of thousands of Naira per project. This business comfortably sustained me through my university years. I was thriving financially and had developed a strong rhythm in executing the work. But as my relationship with God deepened, I began to reflect more critically on the ethical implications of what I was doing. Slowly, a sense of discomfort set in. While I had justified the work initially as a service, I could no longer ignore the fact that I was enabling others to bypass academic integrity. By my final year, I decided to shut the business down.

Even after I stopped, the offers kept coming. People continued to reach out, requesting help with their projects. But I declined each one. The lesson had taken root. I was no longer the same boy who first walked through the gates of the university. I had grown—spiritually, emotionally, and intellectually. I was maturing, and with that growth came a new sense of responsibility and purpose.

The University Debate Champion

As my business grew, my academic performance continued to shine. From the second semester of my third year until graduation, I maintained a straight-A streak at the University of Lagos. In total, I earned 54 As and just 7 Bs over the course of my academic journey. I remained firmly on the University's Scholars List and enjoyed the many benefits that came with it.

Just as I was settling into this rhythm of academic and entrepreneurial success, another opportunity came knocking—one that would, again, stretch me beyond my comfort zone. Like many of the great chances I'd encountered, this one made me uneasy at first. But by now, I had built enough confidence through past victories to know that trying was always worth it.

The call came from the school counsellor's office: the University of Lagos was organizing a campus-wide debate competition to crown the university's greatest debater. A pool of students had been selected to participate, and I had been named the sole representative of the Faculty of Environmental Sciences. The lineup was intimidating. Among the competitors were the best student from Mass Communication, a visually impaired but incredibly articulate gentleman—student union activists known for their fiery public addresses, law students well-versed in the art of argument, and a host of other brilliant minds. Once again, I felt out of place, convinced that I was at a disadvantage.

The first stage of the competition was intense. All twenty of us gathered at the School Council Chambers for an impromptu debate round, coordinated by a distinguished professor from the Department of Mass Communication. Each participant had to draw a card containing a debate topic and a designated position, either for or against. We were given no time to prepare, no room to confer, just three minutes to present our case. It was raw, fast, and demanding. You had to think on your feet and communicate with clarity and conviction, hoping to secure your spot in the next round. I remember the atmosphere was intellectually charged and emotionally intense. It was a test of wit, poise, and the ability to deliver under pressure. And just like many pivotal moments before, I knew that what I did in those few minutes could open yet another door in my evolving journey.

I watched in shock as some of the students I admired most drew their cards and completely froze. They couldn't form coherent arguments, let alone deliver compelling ones. Some started strong but lost steam halfway through. It was a sobering experience. Only those who were brave and well-prepared stood a chance of making it through. A few standout performances, like the gentleman from Mass Communication and another from Engineering, who would later become a close friend made a lasting impression.

When it was my turn, I drew my card, and that's when adrenaline—and I believe the Spirit of God—took over. To this day, I can't remember what topic was on that card, nor the stance I was asked to argue. But I do remember it being the fastest three minutes of my life. I spoke, I delivered—but how I did it is a blur. A few days later, I got word: that twelve people had been eliminated, and I was among the top eight.

Even more exciting, the letter I received placed me in a group with three other finalists for the next stage. We were to meet at the School Counsellor's office for a briefing. There, I met my teammates and learned the topic we would be debating: "University Autonomy—A Positive or Negative?" We were to argue in favour of autonomy.

I have to confess, I was intimidated. The opposing team looked formidable. Their lineup included the Mass Communication star who was also a radio presenter, a vocal student union activist, a charismatic speaker, and a sharp young lady. My team, in contrast, felt mismatched. We had a medical student, a pharmacy student, a science major, and myself. None of us came from disciplines typically known for producing star debaters.

Still, I was chosen as the lead speaker for our team, and I took the role seriously. We exchanged phone numbers and scheduled regular strategy sessions. I dove into research, unpacking everything I could find about university autonomy. I drafted points, honed arguments, and worked late into the night. We rehearsed our delivery, coached one another, and built team chemistry.

I even watched *The Great Debaters* starring Denzel Washington and picked up a few debating tactics from the film. Bit by bit, we transformed into a cohesive unit. There was one more twist: the debate would be broadcast live on UNILAG FM, the university's radio station—which had grown in popularity and now reached an audience well beyond campus.

The night before the debate, we decided to present ourselves as a united front. We agreed on a team dress code: black suits, sky-blue shirts, and navy blue ties. I didn't own a sky blue shirt, so I borrowed one from a cousin who was living with us at the time. It was all coming together. We were the underdogs but we were prepared.

On the day of the debate, the hall was packed. Four professors sat at the judges' table, ready to score the competition. The live broadcast had already begun. As I looked around the room, I didn't recognize a single familiar face. I was up first. I stepped forward, took a deep breath, and opened my argument with a sharp, compelling illustration following a brief yet clever greeting. The audience responded with cheers. From there, I wove together facts, philosophy, and persuasion to build a strong case. It was a solid start, and I knew I had given my team early momentum.

Then came the opposing team's lead speaker—the Mass Communication champion. Guided to the podium by his assistant, he gripped the lectern, leaned into the mic, cleared his throat, and delivered his opening in the most captivating radio voice I had ever heard. The crowd erupted. With every sentence, he drew applause. He was magnetic.

But then, something unexpected happened. The second speaker from my team stepped up to the podium and froze. She lost her train of thought, her composure unravelled, and she left the stage visibly shaken. As the debate continued, I feared we were slipping behind. When the fourth speaker from each team had finished, the judges called on the lead speakers to return to the podium for a three-minute wrap-up. I hadn't prepared for that moment. As I stood to walk up, the teammate who had stumbled earlier squeezed my hand and whispered, "It's in your hands now."

With no time to draft a new argument, I changed tactics. Rather than summarizing our points, I launched into a strategic rebuttal, highlighting the inconsistencies and flaws in the opposing team's logic. It was a gamble. But it worked. In a surprising turn, we won the debate by just one point!. The deciding factor? Our coordinated team attire. The opposing team hadn't bothered, but our matching black suits, sky-blue shirts, and navy blue ties earned us five points. That margin tipped the scale in our favour.

To crown it all, I was named Best Debater at the University of Lagos, another achievement I never could have imagined. As I walked back to my faculty building, word had already spread. My head of department had heard the news and welcomed me back with pride and celebration. It was a moment I'll never forget—a reminder that showing up, standing tall, and staying ready can lead to extraordinary outcomes.

Entrepreneurship, Mindset, and the God Factor

There's something deep within us that stirs when we taste success. It's more than pride—it's a yearning to keep going, to do more, to climb higher. That yearning is the mindset of possibility. Once we glimpse what's achievable, we no longer settle for less. We are wired to pursue growth, and that drive, whether we recognise it or not, is inherently entrepreneurial.

We often think entrepreneurship belongs only to a select few - business founders, tech innovators, or those running start-ups. But the truth is, we are all entrepreneurs in some way. Whether we call ourselves that or not, we live it every day.

I remember asking a group at one of my entrepreneurship workshops, "What's the one word you would use to define entrepreneurship?" The answers came quickly, "opportunity," "risk," "profit," and "problem-solving." Then I asked a second question: "Who here has never dealt with opportunity, risk, or problem-solving in their daily life?" Not a single hand went up.

That's because we all evaluate risk. We identify opportunities. We strategize. We problem-solve. We make bold decisions with no guarantees. These are all hallmarks of entrepreneurship. Life itself is like a startup, and God is our primary investor. He has deposited gifts, talents, and potential in us and it's our job to steward those investments with wisdom and purpose. Looking back at my time at the University of Lagos, two key milestones stand out: starting a successful business as a student and emerging as the university's best debater. At face value, they seem like different achievements. But at the core, they both required the same entrepreneurial elements - the courage to begin, the willingness to embrace uncertainty, and a drive to grow.

These achievements were not the product of talent alone. They were built on mindset, resilience, and most importantly, grace. None of them came easily. There were moments of fear, failure, and doubt. But each win became a stepping stone to the next, affirming that with the right mindset and unwavering faith, what once seemed out of reach could become reality.

Each business breakthrough taught me a lesson that prepared me for the next challenge. Every debate sharpened my thinking and deepened my confidence. Success was never a final destination, it was a compass pointing to even greater potential. This is the power of a growth mindset infused with divine grace. It transforms small beginnings into great achievements. It allows us to see each victory not as an ending, but as a launchpad. When you adopt this mindset and trust in God's leading, limitations fade. What you achieve today is not the ceiling, it's the floor of what's possible tomorrow.

If there's one takeaway from this part of my journey, it's this: success isn't reserved for the chosen few. It's accessible to anyone who dares to grow, thinks creatively, and trusts God's plan. The best is always ahead. More wins lead to more possibilities.

Wisdom Keys from Chapter 6

1. **Success is a Launchpad, Not a Destination** - Every win expands your vision and opens doors to greater possibilities. Instead of seeing success as a finish line, view it as a stepping stone to something even bigger.

2. **Entrepreneurship is First a Mindset:** Opportunity often comes disguised as a challenge. How we see them determines the outcome we get. Those who take action, adapt, and collaborate will always find ways to create value and grow.

3. **Partnerships Unlock Resources and Multiply Impact:** The right partnerships and strategic collaborations provide access to resources, knowledge, and opportunities that one cannot achieve alone. Identifying and working with the right people at the right time can accelerate your success.

4. **Bold Action Turns Ordinary Moments Into Opportunity:** Opportunities rarely announce themselves. It's your willingness to act that reveals them. Trusting in God is essential, but faith must be accompanied by bold steps and sacrifice. When we act on our faith, we position ourselves for divine breakthroughs and limitless growth.

Reflection Questions

1. How do you currently view success? Do you see it as a final destination, or as a springboard to greater achievements?

2. What opportunities have you overlooked because they seemed too small or unexpected? How can you develop an entrepreneurial mindset to seize them?

3. Who are the key people in your life that can help you grow? How can you cultivate stronger, mutually beneficial partnerships?

CHAPTER SEVEN

God's Crucible

"God never uses anyone greatly until He tests them deeply."

- A.W. Tozer.

I once watched a blacksmith at work, hammering away at a glowing piece of metal. The air was thick with heat, and every strike of the hammer sent sparks flying. With each blow, the raw metal shifted, reshaped under relentless pressure. But the process wasn't just about form; it was about strength. The intense fire burned away impurities, leaving behind something purer, stronger, and more resilient. Life often feels like that forge, a place where we are pressed, stretched, and refined by the heat of trials. The weight of challenges can feel unbearable, just as the blacksmith's hammering seemed both excessive and essential. Yet, just as the blacksmith never strikes aimlessly, God is never careless in His refining. Every blow has a purpose. Every moment of pressure is intentional.

Scripture is filled with examples of this divine refining. Think of Joseph - betrayed by his brothers, sold into slavery, falsely accused, and imprisoned, only to rise to prominence as a ruler in Egypt. Or Moses, who spent 40 years in the wilderness before he was ready to lead a nation. Even Jesus, the Son of God, underwent 30 years of preparation for a three-year ministry that transformed the world. Every trial, every season of waiting, every moment of discomfort carries meaning. We often crave ease, shortcuts, and the fast track to our purpose. But just as gold must be refined by fire, and a diamond formed under immense pressure, so too must we pass through the refining hand of God. It is not punishment, it is preparation.

God's crucible, His divine process of refining, shapes us into the people we were always meant to be. No pain is wasted. No struggle is without significance. When we surrender to His hands, we emerge stronger, wiser, and closer to the version of ourselves He envisioned. Just like the metal in the blacksmith's forge, we are being shaped not only for form but for function, not only to shine but to endure. Trust the fire. Trust the process. Trust the One who holds the hammer.

Reflecting on my family background, school years, and university journey, it's now clear that the challenging seasons, the long periods of waiting, and the unexpected detours were far from wasted. They were God's crucible—His refining ground for what was yet to come. But God wasn't done. My dream of travelling abroad remained alive within me, though still blurry around the edges. One thing I clung to was the belief that with a completed first degree, my chances of securing a scholarship for a one-year postgraduate study would be significantly higher.

That goal also aligned with my father's long-standing conviction. Back when I finished secondary school, he believed I wasn't ready for the kind of freedom that life abroad demanded. He wanted me to grow, to mature, and to be forged into a man. That's exactly what my years in Lagos had done for me. God had been in that plan all along, working hand in hand with my father's wisdom. As detailed in earlier chapters, those years shaped something deep and enduring in me. In hindsight, my graduation from the University of Lagos marked more than the end of a chapter, it began a two-year countdown toward the overseas opportunity I had so long desired. It was also the start of another season of preparation. What would unfold during those two years would become yet another defining crucible moment—one God enrolled me into without asking for my permission.

By now, a pattern had emerged in my life. Every time I was on the brink of a new season, God would lead me through an intense stretch of preparation. A crash course of sorts designed to refine my mindset, shape my character, and strengthen my abilities. He never launched me into the unknown unprepared. Whether I recognised it in the moment or not, He was always setting the stage.

One of the most pivotal of those refining seasons would come during my one-year service in the mandatory National Youth Service Corps (NYSC) programme. It was a time that would stretch me, challenge me, and ultimately prepare me for the global stage I had always dreamed of.

The National Youth Service Year: A Divine Crash Course

At first, I saw the NYSC programme as nothing more than a national obligation to get through. But looking back, I now realise it was far more than a bureaucratic rite of passage. It was a divine setup, an accelerated training ground crafted by God for the journey ahead. This season wasn't primarily about building my character; that work had already begun in previous years. Instead, this was a time of deep spiritual development. It was in this season that my faith shifted gears, preparing me for the long, rugged road that lay ahead.

The National Youth Service Corps (NYSC) was established to deploy fresh graduates across different parts of Nigeria, typically far from their state of origin or where they had schooled. The official goal was to encourage national unity and patriotic service in a country divided by ethnic and regional lines. But in reality, for many young people, NYSC had become a year of survival, marked by hardship, adaptation, and life-altering lessons. Though the programme today faces intense criticism for its shortcomings, one profound truth remains: The NYSC was a prophetic fulfilment. A British missionary, Pa S.G. Elton, who mentored several of Nigeria's spiritual fathers, once prophesied, "A time would come when the Nigerian Government would pay the Nigerian youth to preach the gospel in all nooks and crannies of the country." That prophecy came to life in 1973 with the birth of the NYSC scheme.

I was enlisted in the Batch A stream of 2009, and my posting was to Abuja, the Federal Capital Territory of Nigeria. It was one of the most coveted service locations in the country. The reasons were clear: Abuja was the seat of power. If you had the right connections, you could land a posting at a multinational corporation or a top-tier government agency, an ideal launchpad for a stellar career. While Lagos also had its appeal, Abuja had a different allure one rooted in its proximity to national leadership, better quality of life, and more strategic positioning. Across Nigeria, students would pay significant amounts of money to influence their posting to Abuja, though success was never guaranteed. Initially, I was posted to a different state in Northern Nigeria. However, I reached out to a trusted mentor and humbly asked if he could assist in securing a reposting to Abuja. I didn't have the money to fund the move, but he took it upon himself. To my astonishment, I received a second posting letter, this time confirming my relocation to Abuja. I was overwhelmed with joy. Finally, I was stepping out of Lagos to a city where I would be by myself, to carve my path. That, perhaps, was the most thrilling part of the entire posting. A new chapter was about to begin.

About four weeks before I was due to travel to Abuja to begin the mandatory three-week NYSC orientation camp, I was hit with devastating news. On the morning of February 8, 2009, I woke up to find a bulge in my lower left groin. Alarmed, I ran to my dad to show him. One look and he knew exactly what it was—an inguinal hernia. The only remedy? Surgery.

Up until that point, life had been on a high. I had just earned a stellar first-class degree, my future looked bright, and I had received the dream posting to Abuja. In an instant, all of that seemed to hang in the balance. As I later wrote in my book The Parable of the Baker, not even a first-class degree could save me from what was coming. A quick consultation with my dad's surgeon friend confirmed the worst: the hernia was severe and required immediate surgery. I had just 24 hours to transition from packing for a new chapter in Abuja to being prepped for the operating table.

Nothing could have prepared me for the mental and emotional toll of that moment or the psychological rollercoaster of the recovery weeks that followed. But what I didn't realise at the time was that this unexpected crisis was a training ground for what would become a year of multiple, sudden challenges.

Crises, as I've come to learn, are unforgiving in their timing and unrelenting in their demands. Though I had experienced hardship before, this particular challenge was unlike anything I'd faced. It was fast and unfamiliar, and it forced me to adapt with little warning. That's when I realised something profound: crisis moments are crucible moments. They plunge us into three key terrains:

1. **New Terrains**: Encounters with the unfamiliar and unexpected.

2. **Dark Terrains:** Periods marked by loss, pain, or seeming defeat.

3. **Transition Terrains:** Extended seasons of reflection, uncertainty, and waiting.

While I had previously walked through dark and transitional terrains, this health challenge was my first real taste of new terrain, one where I had no control and had to lean entirely on others. The surgery was successful, but the recovery was long and painful. Thankfully, I healed just in time for the Abuja trip, though with strict instructions: no heavy lifting or strenuous activity. In other words, I was told to avoid doing exactly what the orientation camp demanded. Camp life, after all, was known for being physically intense.

Still, I was determined to go. Something deeper in me knew this season had a purpose. I just didn't know yet how much it would change me. Concerned about my health, my dad insisted I travel to Abuja by air. The idea of me enduring a long road trip after surgery was too much for him to bear. In less than an hour, I had landed in Abuja and was on my way to the NYSC orientation camp. Nothing I saw on arrival surprised me, but I was far from mentally prepared.

Camp was a madhouse with thousands of corps members swarming around, trying to navigate the chaos of enrolment. Without completing registration, you couldn't collect your uniforms, secure a mattress, or get assigned to a room. I wheeled my suitcase to the nearest shed, approached a soldier, and asked for directions. As someone who could adapt quickly and make friends easily, I soon connected with others in the same predicament. Together, we tried to navigate the bottlenecks of NYSC bureaucracy. At the heart of camp life was the Mammy Market, a makeshift hub that sprang to life at every NYSC camp.

It was the social and economic centre of camp life. You could find everything there - food, banter, drinks, clothes, barbers, mini-marts. While the government provided meals, they were often barely edible, so those who could afford to eat exclusively at Mammy Market. As always, my friendly nature helped me quickly befriend traders in different stalls.

After a chaotic first day with no progress on my registration and no room assigned, I had to improvise. That night, I slept in Mammy Market, using hard plastic chairs as a makeshift bed, with my suitcase serving as both a pillow and protective barrier. It wasn't glamorous, but it kept my belongings safe. After two nights in Abuja's Harmattan cold, I finally completed my enrolment and secured a room on the third day. But something strange happened that same third day. While waiting to finalize my registration, I was hanging around Mammy Market, chatting with friends and enjoying the vibe. At one point, I wandered near the parade ground where all the military drills took place. A soldier spotted me and demanded to know why I was near the grounds without being in full uniform.

Now, anyone who has experienced NYSC camp knows the soldiers don't play around. They wield enormous authority and regularly dish out harsh punishments. I'd already seen people frog-jumping across the entire field for minor infractions. I knew I couldn't afford to become the next scapegoat. So I panicked and played a trick. I pretended to be deaf and mute. The soldier was stunned when I didn't respond. I mumbled gibberish and took off running, dodging through Mammy

Market. He tried to chase me, but my friends stepped in to shield me. As I ran, I spotted a chapel on the campgrounds, the place where Christian corps members gathered for morning and evening fellowships.

I dashed inside, sat down quickly, and tried to blend in, pretending I'd been there to worship all along. In truth, I had been drifting through camp, enjoying the moment and soaking up the fun of Mammy Market. But God, in His usual way, found a way to redirect me to something greater. That day, I stumbled upon the Nigerian Christian Corpers' Fellowship (NCCF) and my life changed. Only after the soldier gave up the search for me did I finally complete my enrolment. But that moment, panicked, unplanned, and entirely divine marked the beginning of a deeper purpose for my time in Abuja.

Finding NCCF felt like discovering a place of refuge. It was clear that God was sending me a strong message: if I didn't align with His purpose for my time in Abuja, trouble awaited. From that moment on, my carefree life in Mammy Market came to an abrupt end. I still went there to eat occasionally, but the idle hours and constant hanging out stopped. Eventually, I ran out of money and could no longer afford meals at the market, so I started eating the government-provided food, a seeming setback that turned out to be a blessing in disguise.

I had been assigned to Platoon 10, and one of our duties included serving in the camp kitchen. While many of my fellow corps members were content serving food at the front, I took a different route. I volunteered for the back end of kitchen work, scrubbing massive pots by hand, using tin lids to scrape off burnt bits, and cleaning everything for the kitchen staff. The team of about 7 to 10 women who handled the camp meals quickly warmed to me. I became their favourite corps member. My service paid off in unexpected ways. I never had to queue for food again, they always reserved a plate for me, filled with the best portions. For the first time, I saw with my own eyes how service, done sincerely and selflessly, brings its quiet reward.

In the evenings, I began attending fellowship meetings and joined the prayer team of those who interceded for the spiritual direction of the camp. It was during these meetings that I witnessed, for the first time, the demonstration of spiritual gifts. One young woman stood out. She was bold, spiritually intense, and carried herself with unusual confidence. She moved in the prophetic and often shared vivid insights about what she sensed in the spirit. Her name is Lara Shonubi. If any of this sounds strange to you, I completely understand. Up until that point, I hadn't been exposed to this dimension of the Christian faith. I had encountered the Holy Spirit as a child, but I hadn't been in environments where the gifts of the Spirit were actively taught or demonstrated. It was all new.

One evening, after a powerful prayer session, I pulled aside one of the brothers and asked, "What are you guys seeing? I want to see too." He smiled and explained that it was about walking with God and desiring the gifts of the Holy Spirit. God had placed me in a space where He intended to stretch me spiritually, and He began by surrounding me with believers who were ahead of me in their faith walk. Lara, as it turned out, became one of the executives of NCCF and my spiritual mentor during that season. Lara carried gifts I longed for, so I decided to serve her during this period. And if you've followed my story, you know that when I say "serve," I mean giving my all. I made myself available for whatever was needed, at any time. At the same time, I was appointed as the Publicity Secretary of the NCCF Abuja Chapter. Lara and I both became part of the executive committee. But for me, the position was far more than a title. It was my doorway into a vibrant faith community—my access point to the people whose flames would eventually ignite a revival in my own life.

NCCF Family House: Living in the Wilderness

After orientation camp, every corps member is expected to secure accommodation in town, from where they would commute to their place of primary assignment. I hadn't realised this and made no preparations. A few days before the passing-out parade, panic set in. Most of my friends had already paired up and secured places in different parts of Abuja. I had no one left to team up with, and housing in the city was far beyond what I could afford.

Just when I felt stranded, I received a timely and much-needed update: as an executive of the NCCF, I was expected to live in the NCCF Family House. All executive members were required to stay there, alongside other corps members who couldn't afford accommodation in town. The Family House was located on the outskirts of Abuja, precisely in a neighbouring state—Nasarawa State. You can't imagine the relief I felt.

On the final day of camp, we were transported to what would become a sacred space in my journey - a place of spiritual growth, deep friendships, and transformative encounters. I quickly immersed myself in the daily rhythm of the Family House. We held morning and evening devotions, which framed each day in prayer and reflection. After morning devotion, most people would head to their places of primary assignment. But mine had rejected me saying they had already reached their quota of corps members.

In search of an alternative, I reached out to Professor Austin Otegbulu, one of my long-standing mentors from the University of Lagos. He graciously offered me a spot in his private real estate firm's unmanned Abuja office, effectively making me his representative on the ground. Like all corps members, I received a modest government stipend, which sustained me. Occasionally, when he was in town, he would bless me with generous cash gifts. I called them gifts because, truthfully, I didn't close a single sale or lease the entire year. The office was over an hour away, and with the early morning rush-hour traffic, getting there became increasingly difficult. Eventually, I found myself spending more time at the Family House than at the office.

If you've been reading closely, you can probably guess where this is going. That season at the Family House became the training ground for my spiritual development. With time on my hands, I leaned in. I prayed fervently. I learned to hear God's voice. I journaled, studied the Bible, and gave myself wholly to the service of the NCCF especially working closely with Lara whom at this point I called Mama Lara because of her position in the Fellowship. She would entrust crucial duties into my care which I did joyfully, without any complaint. Service was becoming a key that unlocked growth and inner transformation. She often spoke words of blessing over me, prophetic, powerful words that left a lasting mark on my spirit. My only desire was to grow, to serve, to learn, and to become everything God was calling me to be.

As I reflect on those transformative months and flip through the many journals I wrote, I can't help but recognise that this season became a crash course in spiritual leadership. During my service, God began to teach me the Kingdom way of giving. I remember a particular moment clearly. I owned a sleek black suit my dad had bought me from the UK, paired with a lilac shirt and a perfectly matching tie. It was my prized Sunday best. As part of our duties as NCCF executives, we often visited local churches to connect with pastors and build relationships with ministries across the city. They, in turn, would visit and pour into us.

On one such outing, I wore that black suit with pride. I looked good, polished, confident, and ready. During the service, I glanced across the room and noticed our fellowship president. His attire wasn't quite as sharp. At first, I tried to ignore it, brushing it off, but God was speaking. I heard a gentle prompting in my spirit: "Can you see your president's dressing?"

"Huh?" I responded silently.

Then it came again—clearer this time. "You should make your president look good. When you get home, give him everything you're wearing."

I froze. That one instruction sparked a fierce internal debate. "What if this isn't God?" I wondered. "Won't he be embarrassed? What if he refuses it?"

But that evening before our prayer time, the conviction only deepened. I had been taught that delayed obedience is still disobedience. So, I swallowed my doubts, approached him, and told him what God had laid on my heart. I handed over the suit, shirt, and tie. He accepted them graciously and prayed for me, and I felt both the sting of parting with something precious and the peace that comes from obedience.

That moment became a defining foundation for my life of giving and service. I began to understand generosity not as obligation, but as worship. That same season also saw me joining mission trips to remote villages with the Fellowship spreading the gospel and meeting the needs of unreached communities. My faith was no longer abstract. It was becoming a lived experience.

It was also during this profound season that I met Rev. Sam Oye, the man who would become my pastor and spiritual father. Our first encounter was as memorable as it was unexpected. As an executive team, we paid a courtesy visit to his church at Owenna House. I was used to seeing high-profile pastors step out in suits and polished shoes. But when Rev. Sam emerged, he wore a simple shirt, jeans, and sneakers. His humility struck me before he ever said a word. But when he opened his mouth, everything changed. His wisdom, clarity, and spiritual authority poured out in ways that left me stunned. I wanted to hear more. And yet, throughout that meeting, I sat near the back. Then came the surprise. After he finished speaking, Rev. Sam walked past the front rows, came to the back where I was seated, and looked straight at me. "What's your name?" he asked.

"Adeyinka Adewale," I replied, startled.

He smiled. "I want you to keep in touch with me. There's so much inside of you."

I was floored. He gave me his number, and with that, a divine door opened. That moment marked the beginning of one of the most meaningful relationships in my life. Rev. Sam became God's gift to me especially because, though I didn't know it yet, I was less than two years away from losing my biological father. God, in His foresight, had already positioned another father figure to walk with me. Since that day, Rev. Sam has spoken over my life and offered guidance through every major decision I've faced from career to marriage to ministry. Through him, I've come to understand just how intentional God is about placing the right people in our lives at the right time.

For me, the one-year NYSC service became a crucible, a season where God was breaking, moulding, and refining me for what lay ahead. At first, it felt like being thrown into the deep end. The unfamiliar environment, the diverse people, the new expectations—it was overwhelming. But beneath the surface of discomfort, God was at work. He used the unfamiliar to stretch my adaptability. He used the solitude to deepen my dependence on Him. He used the responsibilities to sharpen my leadership and build resilience. It reminded me of David's journey. Before he ever faced Goliath or ascended to the throne, he spent years in obscurity, tending sheep in the wilderness. It was there he learned to fight off lions and bears, skills that would later prepare him for the giant he would one day face. In the same way, my time in the NYSC programme was not just about fulfilling a national obligation; it was a divinely orchestrated training ground for the battles and breakthroughs ahead.

There were days I asked God, "Why am I here? Why does this have to be so hard?" But through those questions, I grew. As Maya Angelou once said, "I can be changed by what happens to me. But I refuse to be reduced by it." That became the theme of my service year. I was being changed, stretched, and strengthened, but I refused to let the process break me.

By the time that season came to an end, I was no longer the person who had walked into it. I had developed a deeper well of perseverance, a clearer sense of purpose, and a more intimate trust in God's process. What I once viewed as a compulsory rite of passage had become one of the most defining chapters of my life.

God's crucible is rarely comfortable, but it is always necessary. If we let Him, He will use every season, especially the challenging ones, to prepare us for what's next. He doesn't refine us to punish us. He does it to strengthen us, purify us, and make us ready for the future He's carefully shaping.

What I didn't know at the time was that another test, far bigger than anything I had yet encountered was waiting just around the corner.

How to Posture During Crucible Seasons

Crucible seasons come in many forms. For one person, it might be serving under a difficult boss. For another, it could be a prolonged season of waiting, financial lack, academic failure, a personal health challenge, or the loss of a loved one. Whatever shape they take, one thing is clear: crucible moments are not random. They are divinely orchestrated seasons with specific assignments - God's way of preparing us for the weight of what lies ahead.

As I look back on my crucible seasons, from my surgery before NYSC camp to serving with almost nothing in Abuja, to losing the comforts I had taken for granted, I realise these were all sacred appointments. And if there's one thing I've learned, it's that our posture during these moments is everything. How we respond can determine whether we come out bitter or better, hardened or refined.

1. **Trust the One Who Shapes You:** Above all else, trust the God who is holding the chisel. The pain may be real, the process uncomfortable, but the Potter never takes His eyes off the clay. He knows exactly what He's shaping you into. When David was in the wilderness, he couldn't have imagined he was being trained to become king. Yet every bear he fought and every lonely night with the sheep was a part of his preparation.

2. **Embrace a Heart of Service:** Nothing realigns our hearts faster than service. When we shift the focus from ourselves to others, something powerful happens, we stop seeing our pain as punishment and start recognising it as purpose. My time serving in the kitchen, walking in the heat to buy food for Lara, or doing behind-the-scenes tasks nobody noticed, broke the back of selfishness in me. Service helps birth strength. It re-centres our hearts and aligns us with heaven's priorities.

3. **Don't Despise Small Beginnings:** It might feel like what you're doing now is insignificant, but in God's eyes, no act of faithfulness is ever wasted. Washing pots, praying quietly, showing up daily with a good attitude—these are the things that build spiritual muscle. They prepare you for the platforms you've been praying for.

4. **Develop Spiritual Discernment:** In the crucible, God speaks. Often not in thunderclaps or lightning bolts, but in whispers, nudges, promptings, and inner convictions. Learning to discern His voice is critical in these seasons. It may come through Scripture, a mentor, or even a seemingly random

instruction like giving away a beloved suit. Train your heart to listen.

5. Journal the Journey: One of the most powerful tools during my NYSC season was journaling. Writing helped me make sense of what God was doing. It allowed me to trace patterns, capture insights, and preserve moments of revelation. Your crucible season is a classroom, document the lessons.

6. Build the Right Relationships: No one walks through the fire alone. Surround yourself with people who speak life, remind you of who you are, and challenge you to keep going. In my case, it was people like Lara and Rev. Sam who became divine reinforcements in my season of refinement.

7. Choose Obedience Over Comfort: Sometimes the instructions will stretch you—giving something away, serving without being noticed, remaining in a hard place. Obedience in the crucible is never easy, but it is always fruitful. Your yes to God will echo beyond your season of fire.

In the end, crucible moments are not meant to break you. They are meant to remake you. They strip away what's not needed and strengthen what is essential. And when it's all said and done, you'll look back and realise that God wasn't just taking you through something—He was building someone. You.

Wisdom Keys from Chapter 7

1. **Every Challenge is a Refining Process:** Like a blacksmith's fire purifies metal, life's trials are not meant to break us but to shape us. Hardships are not punishments; they are preparation for a greater calling.

2. **Crisis Moments Reveal New Terrains:** Difficult seasons introduce us to unfamiliar challenges some expose our weaknesses, some test our patience, and others prepare us for transitions. How we navigate them determines our growth.

3. **Service and Submission Unlock Unexpected Blessings:** True growth happens when we humble ourselves to serve others. Serving with sincerity whether in leadership, faith, or friendships opens doors we never imagined and accelerates our spiritual and personal development.

4. **God's Preparation is Always Ahead of Your Next Season:** Before every major transition, God places us in a "training ground" to equip us for what's ahead. Recognizing and embracing these seasons of preparation allows us to step into new opportunities fully prepared.

Reflection Questions

1. Have you ever faced a challenge that felt unbearable at the time but later turned out to be a necessary preparation for something greater? What did you learn from it?

2. In what ways have you resisted or struggled with seasons of refinement in your life? How can you shift your mindset to embrace them instead?

3. How can you intentionally serve and grow in the relationships and opportunities God has placed before you? What small act of service can you commit to today?

CHAPTER EIGHT

The Darkest Hours and The Triumph of Faith

"Faith is the bird that feels the light when the dawn is still dark."

- Rabindranath Tagore.

There are seasons in life we know will come yet are never fully prepared for. There are moments in life when darkness seems unrelenting, when grief, uncertainty, and pain threaten to consume every bit of strength we have left. It is in these moments that our faith is tested and refined. The loss of a loved one, the sudden collapse of what was once stable, and the burden of caring for someone who once cared for us can shake us to our very core. But within these trials lies an extraordinary truth: darkness, no matter how overwhelming will not last forever. If our faith does not fail, we will always triumph. But the ultimate triumph I have come to appreciate is to emerge on the other side of our dark seasons with a renewed sense of purpose, hope, and divine preparation for greater things to come.

The Brewing Storm

My time in Abuja ended remarkably. Beyond the crash course in spiritual growth, I also emerged as one of the most celebrated corps members in the city. I served in one of the Community Development Service (CDS) centres focused on the Millennium Development Goals (MDGs), and took on a full-scale project to educate secondary school students and renovate their classrooms. That effort earned me the award of Best MDG Youth Corps Advocate in the state. Once again, as God would have it, honour followed diligence, and I was reminded that the journey to Abuja was not only about spiritual formation but also about fruitful impact.

With a sense of fulfilment and anticipation, I returned to Lagos to begin the next chapter—finding a job and building my post-NYSC life. But no sooner had I arrived than something strange and deeply unsettling began to unfold. My father, who had always been razor-sharp and strong-willed, suddenly began showing signs of cognitive decline at an alarming pace. Alarmed and confused, I sat him down to ask a few questions, only to realise he was struggling to respond coherently. Panic surged through me and with the help of key family members, we got him to the hospital. It was there I learned the devastating news that my dad had stage 4 prostate cancer. The disease had metastasized throughout his body, and the symptoms we were now witnessing were its cruel effects.

Within a short period, my father lost his ability to speak well. My life changed overnight. Instead of planning my future or applying for jobs, I found myself driving to the hospital at the crack of dawn to register his name for cancer treatment, rushing home to get him ready, and driving him to the hospital for his appointments. This became my new routine. My entire world was upended. Becoming the primary caregiver to my father was emotionally jarring. Here was the man who had raised me, strong, proud, and fiercely independent now fully reliant on me for his basic needs. I felt woefully unprepared. Many nights, I cried silently, asking God why I was in this place. Why now? Why me? But in the same breath, I remembered: that God had given me the grace to serve. So I leaned into it. I gave my all to care for my father, supported by family during this trying time. As a result, everything else in my life paused. I couldn't job hunt. I couldn't plan for the future. My entire focus had become one thing: serving my father.

In the months that followed, he thankfully recovered, but he soon faced another medical crisis. He had a fall that resulted in another few months in an orthopaedic hospital, leading to more back-and-forth hospital visits. At the end of this ordeal, I realized that God, in His wisdom, had prepared me for this season of hardship. The way I nursed my father could only have been possible because God had given me a heart of service. The way I endured the emotional turmoil of seeing my father in such a vulnerable state could only have come from the strong faith God had instilled in me a few months prior through my one-year NYSC program. There was much more that had gone into preparing me for these moments that would become some of the most difficult of my life. After his recovery, he regained his mobility and was able to return to work part-time. At this time, I was also fortunate to secure a job at a property development company. The CEO of the company, a good Christian and a man I grew to admire became another professional mentor to me.

Although my stay in the organisation was short, I demonstrated my commitment by rewarding him with my very best in creativity, passion, and excellence. During this period also, I applied for my master's program in the United Kingdom. I received a couple of full scholarships, but I could not accept them because my father was still ill, and I did not know when he would be well enough for me to leave. By this time, my responsibility of being his primary caregiver was easing because he and recovered and I was able to work. A few months later, I received an admission offer from the University of Reading to study for a master's in International Management. When I shared the news with my father, he gave me his blessing and released me. His blessing meant the world to me because my dream of studying abroad for my postgraduate degree was finally materializing, and this time, I had his full support.

The University of Reading Chronicles

I arrived the United Kingdom in the early morning of September 15, 2010. My maternal uncle, Uncle Kunle Ojo, the only relative I had in the country at the time had arranged a ride to pick me up from the airport. I spent a few weeks with his family acclimating to the weather and adjusting to a new pace of life. The weekend before school began, he drove me to the

University of Reading, where I checked into my hostel accommodation. Life in the UK was different from what I had imagined. I suddenly found myself alone in a room, navigating a new country, a new system, unfamiliar weather, and the stark reality of independence. One of the most notable changes was access to high-speed internet all day long, something I had never experienced before. That freedom, though exhilarating, became one of the sternest tests of my discipline and devotion to God.

I began my journey at Henley Business School with a single-minded goal: to finish with a distinction and honour the faith my father had placed in me. Before leaving Nigeria, I had called Reverend Dr Sam Oye, who prayed for me and said something I'll never forget: he believed strongly that God was sending me to the UK for a bigger mission and challenged me to deliver nothing but the best results. I was familiar with such missions. My time in Abuja during the NYSC had spiritually grounded me, preparing me to face my father's illness and the pressures of caregiving.

So, I began my studies in Reading with enthusiasm, passion, and determination. I made good friends and built strong relationships with lecturers and university alumni, many of whom became mentors. These mentors played a key role in helping me adapt to the British educational system. While my background at the University of Lagos had given me a solid foundation, excelling in the UK demanded something different: critical thinking. It was a humbling masterclass in adaptation. I quickly learned that success in a new context requires the ability to unlearn and relearn. Thankfully, God placed the right people in my life to guide me.

Beyond academics, I knew I had to find my spiritual footing. That was when I discovered the Reading University Bible Study Society. The founders, Pastor Mike and Celina Adeyemi, would later become my spiritual leaders at Christ Abundant Life Ministries (CALM), our local assembly in Reading. Initially, I joined the Bible study group simply to grow in faith. I wasn't keen on taking on any leadership roles. My focus was on excelling academically, adjusting to a new country, and mastering critical thinking and analytical writing. I didn't want any distractions. At one Wednesday meeting, Pastor Celina called me aside to pray for me. After the prayer, she said, "My son, I feel very strongly that God wants you to serve in this fellowship." I smiled politely and said, "Thank you so much, ma'am—but no thanks." Despite my history of service, I hesitated. I was unsure how to balance responsibility with the academic demands of my programme.

I promised to pray about it, but deep down, I already knew the answer. When I pray about things I already know I should do, God often responds not with words but with conviction. The following Wednesday, I considered skipping Bible study altogether to watch movies and relax but my heart wasn't at peace. Eventually, I walked 35 minutes in the cold to the fellowship. That evening, I said yes to service again. That "yes" would turn into four years of meritorious service, teaching the Word diligently and faithfully. Today, as I pastor a congregation in the UK, I look back and realise those Bible study years were a crash course in pastoral leadership. Once again, I saw the hand of God preparing me for the future, shaping me in the hidden places.

Beyond Bible study and church, I was also active in community service, earning recognition from the University of Reading. I joined the Africa Christian Fellowship (ACF), drawn to the quality of minds in the group, many of whom had completed PhDs at the university. Those years in Reading became some of the most cherished of my life. While I thrived academically, I was also being shaped in leadership. My leadership training extended into secular spaces too. I co-founded the Reading University Nigerian Students' Society (RUNSS) with a good friend. As its first president, I found myself wearing two hats—spiritual and secular—leading both in the church and on campus. This dual experience became foundational to my understanding of the Christian life: we are called to lead in both sacred and secular spaces. Our influence should transcend walls, touching lives, building communities, and pointing people to the light of Christ wherever we go.

The Darkest Hours

During my master's program in International Management, I deliberately chose a dissertation topic that would allow me to return to Lagos, Nigeria, for data collection. But more than that, I longed to see my father, whom I hadn't seen in nearly eight months. That trip became more than just academic, it became deeply personal. I travelled back to Lagos, completed my research, and cherished every moment I spent with my dad. Though it lifted my spirits to see him resuming parts of his routine such as visiting construction sites and occasionally making it to the office, I couldn't ignore how frail he had become. Something inside me was unsettled, even as I smiled through our conversations.

My final moments with him are forever etched in my heart. He had purchased my return ticket to the UK for August 2, 2011. Though his cancer had started creeping back, he never told me. On the evening of my departure, he called me into his room. With a heavy voice, he told me he wished he had the strength to accompany me to the airport but trusted I'd understand why he couldn't. That was our last conversation—one that ended with his blessing. Those words would come to mean everything to me.

I turned back to wave goodbye; that would be the last time I saw my father.

Just weeks after returning to the UK, his health deteriorated rapidly. He was admitted to a teaching hospital. Then, one fateful morning, I received the dreaded phone call from my brother: my dad had passed away. At that moment, it felt like my world came crashing down. I had lost not just my father, but my best friend. I sat by the roadside, weeping uncontrollably until I was picked up by a pastor couple— Pastor Jire and Pastor Funke, who became an immense source of comfort in that dark season and the ones that followed.

Despite the heartbreak, I found some peace knowing my father had seen my academic results before he passed. He knew I was on track to graduate with distinction, pending the submission of my dissertation. That gave me a quiet sense of fulfilment. He had lived to see me pursue and thrive in the dream he had helped shape, the dream of academic excellence that had always been so important to him. After his passing, I completed my program at the University of Reading with distinction and received special recognition for meritorious community service. I dedicated the award to my father, who had taught me the value of service, the pursuit of excellence, and the importance of doing everything with heart.

The Turning Point

Life after Henley Business School took an unexpected turn. I had originally planned to return to Nigeria, but my father's death changed everything. I had to pivot to my Plan B - to pursue a PhD, something I had always dreamed of. But that raised difficult questions: How would I fund it? Where would the scholarship come from? And, most immediately, where would I live?

At this critical juncture, God sent help again. Pastor Jire and his wife, Pastor Funke—who was completing his PhD at the time—opened their home to me. They gave me a place to stay for a full year, completely free of charge. In one of the hardest seasons of my life, their kindness and generosity became a shelter for me—both literally and emotionally. I will forever be grateful for their support and the role they played in helping me find my footing again.

I explored various options for travelling to Canada or the United States, feeling unsure about my next steps. One evening, I reached out to Reverend Sam, who had become one of my closest confidants and shared my plans with him. Without hesitation, he responded with conviction: "I sense very strongly that God still has a purpose for you in the United Kingdom. Don't go. Stay." Respecting his insight, I chose to follow his counsel.

Two weeks later, something remarkable happened. I had stepped out of the library, where I spent nearly every day, to take a brief walk. Despite the uncertainty that surrounded my life at the time, I found solace and fulfilment in serving with the Bible Study Society. Teaching Bible study on Tuesdays, assisting with church vigils on Fridays, and coordinating Sunday services became my lifelines, bringing peace and joy amidst challenging circumstances.

On a particular evening, as I entered the Henley Business School building, I unexpectedly encountered one of my former professors. Surprised but delighted to see me, she asked about my current situation and plans. As I shared my predicament, she expressed genuine sympathy, then surprised me further by asking if I'd considered pursuing a PhD. Given Reverend Sam's recent guidance and my longstanding dream of earning a doctorate, I immediately seized the opportunity. Within days, I submitted a research proposal as she had instructed.

A few weeks later, I received an astonishing letter—confirmation that I had been awarded a full scholarship for a PhD in Leadership, Organizations, and Behaviour at Henley Business School, valued at £100,000. At that moment, I recalled a pivotal event from a few years earlier when God had instructed me to give away some surplus funds from a university seminar as scholarships to indigent students. Now, that seed I had obediently sown was returning to me exponentially multiplied. The contrast between the modest 60,000 naira I had given and the immense value of this new scholarship was impossible to miss. It was yet another testament to the incredible power of obedience.

The profound lesson here is clear: life often presents opportunities in seed form, and wisdom lies in recognizing the seed and choosing to sow rather than consume it. A seed unsown can never yield a harvest. Yet, if we patiently delay gratification and invest our seed, it eventually returns to us, often in ways and measures far beyond our imagination. Reflecting deeply, I realized that my previous experiences had all been purposeful preparations by God. Had He not strengthened my faith during my formative season in Abuja, I might have collapsed under the immense pressures I faced later. It became clear to me how intentional God is carefully shaping, moulding, and refining us for the trials ahead. He does not only equip us for service; He fortifies us to withstand storms and persevere through adversity.

Emerging from these trials, I understood that God had been present all along, fully aware of the challenges I would face and actively preparing me to endure and triumph. It was in that transformative season that the wisdom for my first book, "The Parable of the Baker," was conceived. Using the metaphor of baking, I illustrated how life serves as God's oven—a place where He refines us, shaping us into something remarkable, prepared to impact the world.

Navigating your Darkest Hours with 'ACES': A Practical Guide

Grief can be very hard on us, plunging us into darkness. Through my journey in processing my grief, I found guidance through the wisdom in Scripture and research. I learned practical steps to navigate such seasons victoriously with a compass I called ACES:

1. A - Anchor Your Trust in God

In your darkest moments, remind yourself that God is in control and trustworthy, even when circumstances suggest otherwise. Proverbs 3:5-6 encourages us, "Trust in the Lord with all your heart and lean not on your own understanding; in all your ways acknowledge Him, and He shall direct your paths." Paul's submission in Romans 8:28 also became an anchor, that all things work together for our good because we love God and are called according to His purpose. During my dad's illness, trusting God's sovereignty helped me find peace and strength amidst the chaos. It is usually hard to find any good in darkness, that's why we need an anchor for our souls to mitigate against drifting into the abyss.

2. C- Cultivate an Attitude of Gratitude

Research from positive psychology confirms that gratitude can significantly improve mental and emotional well-being during tough times. 1 Thessalonians 5:18 advises, "Give thanks in all circumstances." By intentionally choosing gratitude, you create space for joy and resilience to grow in the face of adversity. Gratitude can also inspire us towards serving others during our struggles to shift our focus outward, breaking the chains of self-pity and despair. My dedication to the Bible Study Society and church service during uncertain times in Reading brought joy and purpose. Serving others builds resilience, renews strength, and often reveals God's deeper purposes.

3. E - Embrace a Posture of Prayer and Reflection

Prayer isn't merely a spiritual practice; it's a lifeline during trials. Philippians 4:6–7 instructs us, "Do not be anxious about anything, but in every situation, by prayer and petition, with thanksgiving, present your requests to God." In my moments of despair, consistent prayer provided clarity, comfort, and assurance of God's presence. I expressed my concerns and grievances to God, who hears me without judging me. I took courage from the book of Psalms where a lot of heartfelt reflection and prayers were written. I had the permission to do the same.

4. **S - Seek Community and Wise Counsel**

You cannot endure dark seasons alone. Surround yourself with people who can support, guide, and pray with you. Ecclesiastes 4:9–10 emphasizes, "Two are better than one... if either of them falls down, one can help the other up." During my challenging transition after losing my father, the support from the people around especially my mentors and pastors was invaluable.

In conclusion, your darkest hours are not the end; they are stepping stones toward greater victories. Embrace trust, prayer, community, service, obedience, gratitude, and purpose. Hold onto faith, for triumph awaits beyond the darkness.

Wisdom Keys from Chapter 8

1. Seasons of Pain are Doors to a Greater Purpose: Life's darkest moments are often the training grounds for greater assignments. Just as my faith was strengthened through hardships, our trials are not pointless; they refine and prepare us for bigger responsibilities in the future.

2. Obedience to God Unlocks Unexpected Blessings: Sacrifices made in obedience to God are never wasted. The seed sown in faith—whether time, resources, or service—eventually returns in multiplied blessings.

3. Serving in the Waiting Season Brings Clarity and Breakthrough: In seasons of uncertainty, it is easy to feel stuck. However, rather than staying idle or discouraged, choosing to serve can be the key to unlocking the next phase of life. Even when faced with uncertainty about the future, I poured himself into service, and in doing so, God aligned my steps.

4. God's Preparation is Intentional: Every challenge, success, and experience in life is a piece of God's grand design. He equips us with the strength, faith, and resilience needed for future challenges. Nothing is random; God is always working behind the scenes, shaping us for what lies ahead.

Reflection Questions

1. How have the trials in your life shaped you for the better? Reflect on a difficult season and identify the lessons and strengths you gained from it.

2. What seeds of obedience are you being called to sow today? Consider an act of sacrifice - whether in service, generosity, or commitment that God may be nudging you to take, even when it seems inconvenient.

3. Are you fully trusting God's process, even when the outcome is unclear? Examine whether you are resisting a season of preparation or embracing it with faith, knowing that God is leading you toward a greater purpose.

CHAPTER NINE

Moulding Lives, Building Nations: A Life of Purpose and Service

"Unless we lose ourselves in service to others, there is little purpose to our own lives."

- Thomas Monson

From the moment I turned eighteen and began engaging deeply with transformative books and insightful mentors, my awareness of God's purpose for my life intensified. Through prayerful reflection and careful observation, I discovered the driving force behind my existence: a passionate desire to mould lives and build nations. This wasn't merely a slogan or abstract ideal, it became the foundational principle guiding every action and decision I made, fuelled by an unwavering commitment to service, empowerment, and lasting impact.

This clarity emerged gradually, as I carefully traced the common threads woven throughout my life experiences. My passion for serving others was never accidental; rather, it was intentionally shaped by my upbringing, my family background, and firsthand encounters with the unmet needs of those around me. Growing up, I observed countless individuals brimming with potential yet lacking the opportunities or guidance necessary to realize their greatness. I witnessed how a simple act of support could redirect the trajectory of someone's life, how an encouraging word could reignite lost hope, and how genuine leadership transcends power—it is fundamentally about empowering others. These powerful insights gave birth to my philosophy of servant leadership, placing the needs and development of others at the very heart of all my endeavours.

My belief has always been simple yet profound: building a great nation begins with nurturing great individuals. Transforming individual lives inevitably uplifts societies, and empowering people strengthens entire communities. Whether mentoring young people, creating opportunities for those in need, or advocating for meaningful societal changes, I have consistently viewed leadership as an opportunity to serve, rather than to be served.

Throughout my journey, I have been privileged to touch lives, guiding others to discover their strengths, overcome personal limitations, and confidently pursue their dreams. Each moment of impact, each story of transformation, and every changed life reinforces my conviction that our true legacy lies not in what we accumulate but in the lives we positively influence. The profound benefits of serving others have become so evident to me that I actively teach this principle as a core component of my mentoring programmes.

I will delve deeper into this deeply-held philosophy, sharing how my commitment to moulding lives and building nations has shaped my life's work. This philosophy is more than just an approach; it is a call to action, a mindset, and a profound responsibility. When we lift others, we do more than transform individual destinies, we shape the trajectory of entire generations.

How Excellent Service Earned Me My First Trip Abroad

For everything I have mentioned so far in this book, particularly regarding travelling abroad, my trip to the United Kingdom was not my first. My first trip abroad came in 2006, during my time at the University of Lagos. At the height of my journey there, I had continued to demonstrate not only academic excellence but also a commitment to service and great work.

You may recall that I built strong relationships with remarkable individuals within the university system. One of them was the then Dean of the Faculty of Environmental Sciences, Professor Igwe. Professor Igwe became a father figure to me, he was amiable, kind, and always encouraging me in my scholarly pursuits. I was pleasantly surprised to see such a great leader exhibit such humility, and he quickly became one of the most influential figures of my time at the University of Lagos.

I remember one of our usual conversations. Whenever he arrived at the faculty, I would run to greet him, take his bag, and help carry it to his office. During one of these interactions, he mentioned a lady who was aspiring to set up a travel agency and expected a large portion of her market to come from University of Lagos students. She wanted a full-scale market survey conducted on the university campus and was looking for a competent hand to execute the job.

Since I had built my business around executing such projects, and earning a good income from them, I told the Dean to connect me with her. I was more than delighted to take on the task. He was pleased that I was both willing and capable of handling the project because he trusted me to do an outstanding job, as I was one of his scholars.

I had a fruitful meeting with the lady. She explained the scope of the work, and I assured her I would get it done. I designed a comprehensive market survey questionnaire, recruited a few assistants, and collected data from over 200 students. I then analysed the data using data analysis software and compiled a detailed report highlighting my findings and recommendations on how she could position her business in the market. One additional survey I conducted, which she hadn't initially requested, was a willingness-to-pay analysis among students. This turned out to be a game changer, as it helped her determine the ideal price points that students were willing to pay for travel services. The CEO was so impressed with the quality of my work that she told the Dean she couldn't have received a better report even if she had hired a top professional to do the job.

At this point, we had never discussed any form of remuneration. The Dean was like a father to me, and I never intended to charge for the work. To me, it was an act of service, an opportunity to contribute to a worthy venture. To my surprise, I received an email from the CEO of the company informing me that, in appreciation of my excellent service, I would be granted an all-expenses-paid trip to Dubai for one week. I was in complete shock when I read the email. I rushed to my dad and said, "Daddy, I have been given a fully paid trip to Dubai because of a project I carried out on campus!" He was overjoyed for me. Shortly after, I received my air ticket, hotel reservation, and e-visa to Dubai via email after submitting my passport details. It felt like a dream. My father further supported my trip by giving me some extra hundreds of dollars for the journey. Before I knew it, I was on my way to Dubai—my first solo trip outside Nigeria.

My father saw me off at the airport and gave me some candid advice to be careful with the food I ate on the aircraft. But as someone eager to experience everything offered, I ate every meal I was served! Upon arrival, I checked into my hotel and embarked on one of the most memorable experiences of my life. The CEO of the company had not only paid for my trip but had also scheduled specific experiences for each day, allowing me to fully explore Dubai. This was as far back as 2007 when Dubai was still undergoing massive development, but the Burj Al Arab was already standing—a magnificent architectural feat. I remember standing in front of the building, staring at it, and seeing endless possibilities in my mind. That trip to Dubai became a defining moment in my life. It expanded my vision beyond my present challenges and gave me significant exposure to what I could become and achieve if only I applied myself and looked beyond my immediate circumstances.

Once again, excellence had opened doors for me. Delivering excellent work and service earned me yet another great honour, proving that diligence, service, and excellence never go unrewarded.

My Foray into Social Innovation

The trip to Dubai opened my eyes to how visionary leadership could transform the trajectory of an entire generation, making a country one of the most desirable destinations on earth. Now, in 2025, Dubai remains one of the most sought-after destinations for holidays and sightseeing. Today, more skyscrapers have emerged, even taller than the Burj Al Arab, each representing groundbreaking architectural feats that attract visitors from around the world. The transformation of Dubai from a desert landscape into a global tourism and business hub inspired me to reimagine the possibilities for my community.

When I returned to Lagos, I looked around the slum community where I lived at the time Iwaya community, The waterfront, which was then used as a refuse dump, could be something much greater. I began to envision how Iwaya could become not just a place where young people found hope but a thriving environment where tourism and community development could flourish.

This realization led me into the world of social innovation. My first set of investigations examined how delinquent young people in the community could be rehabilitated and transformed into productive citizens. The findings from my research became a full-blown conference paper, which I later presented at the University of Lagos to a full house. The paper was met with much appreciation, not just from academics and scholars but also from local community leaders who saw the potential impact of my ideas.

Going beyond this, I became one of the most active engagement experts on the UN Voices of Youth platform. This exposure propelled me to seek greater opportunities to showcase how a community like Iwaya could be transformed into a thriving, vibrant environment. This led to exciting opportunities with the United Nations Habitat, which at the time had published a report on slum communities in Nigeria. My community, Iwaya, was listed as one of those communities. Instead of merely observing this report, I decided to act. As someone who had lived in the community and had become adept at conducting research there, I knew I had a voice to contribute. With the help of local chiefs and community leaders, whom I built strong alliances with, I was able to write position papers that were later sent to the United Nations Habitat. One of these papers was eventually accepted for presentation at a United Nations Habitat Conference in China.

This was another significant milestone, a testament to how persistence, excellence, and the willingness to engage my mind were shaping my future. However, despite securing a visa and having my father's financial support, I could not attend the conference due to a scheduling conflict with my final year project defence at the University of Lagos. Although the trip to China did not materialize, it ignited a deep-seated desire in me to see slum communities transformed into thriving, self-sustaining environments.

This period also sharpened my awareness of my environment and deepened my passion for mentoring young people, building them into future leaders, and collaborating with stakeholders to drive meaningful change. I realized that true transformation in communities starts with the empowerment of young minds. I recall that, without being asked, I began visiting local schools in Iwaya, offering to give motivational talks to students. The teachers and principals of these schools welcomed me with open arms, allowing me to tour different schools over several weeks to inspire students and help them see possibilities beyond their immediate circumstances. At the time, I was just a young university student trying to find my footing. However, I recognized the advantage I had, I was already at the University of Lagos, a feat that many young people in my community only dreamed of achieving.

Seeing this gap, I decided to use my university experience as a platform for inspiration. I wanted to plant the seeds of ambition and possibility in the minds of younger students. I spoke to them about believing in themselves, about dreaming beyond their surroundings, and about the power of education to unlock doors they never thought possible. This commitment to youth empowerment became yet another foundational pillar for the greater things that lay ahead in my journey.

Much like my experience in Iwaya, similar social innovation efforts have transformed disadvantaged communities worldwide:

- **Makoko Floating School (Nigeria):** Architect Kunle Adeyemi designed a floating school to help children in Lagos' Makoko slum access education despite flooding challenges. This initiative, like my vision for Iwaya, sought to reimagine possibilities for marginalized communities.

- **Kibera Slum Upgrading Project (Kenya):** This initiative focused on transforming one of Africa's largest slums through education, housing, and sanitation improvements, showing that dedicated community engagement can lead to lasting change.

- **The Favelas of Rio de Janeiro (Brazil):** Social enterprises and government-led efforts have turned some of Brazil's infamous slums into vibrant cultural and economic centres through community-driven solutions.

These examples affirm that no community is beyond transformation - it only takes vision, persistence, and a commitment to creating opportunities for those who need them most. In retrospect, my early days of social innovation, engagement in research, and commitment to mentoring youth all became stepping stones that later shaped my larger aspirations for community transformation on a global scale. It all started with a belief in the power of change and the courage to act on that belief.

Turning a Full Circle

During this time, something deeper was being formed within me, something stronger than just the work I was doing. I was developing and cultivating a strong mindset for leadership and organizational transformation. This would later become one of the defining pillars of my work as an Associate Professor of Leadership, Ethics, and Entrepreneurship and as a pastor of a thriving church community in London.

At the point when I got employed at Henley Business School after my PhD, I remember being approached by someone I now refer to as my brother from another mother, Jean-Pierre Choulet. Jean-Pierre shared with me the vision that Henley was pursuing in West Africa—a mission to build the people who will build the businesses that will build Africa. He asked if I was on board. It was like asking a fish if it wanted to swim or asking a lion if it wanted meat for lunch. The vision was so aligned with my identity and passion that I immediately seized the opportunity. Together, we travelled to Lagos to begin this work.

Upon our arrival, we were met at the airport by our host, Sam Immanuel, the founder of Semicolon Africa. As we sat at the airport, Sam began sharing his journey with me—how he left Silicon Valley in the United States to return to Nigeria and start a software engineering institute. His vision was to train young people with technical and life skills to fill a rapidly growing market need for software engineers and digital innovators. In a world that was becoming increasingly digital, and with Africa housing the largest youth population, it was a no-brainer to build a system that transformed young Africans from mere consumers of digital technology into skilled participants and contributors.

As I listened to Sam, it was as if he was speaking my language. We belonged to the same tribe of thinkers and doers. Without hesitation, I said yes to him, yes to Jean-Pierre, and yes to the mission. I was ready to do anything within my capacity to help Semicolon Africa realize its vision. That marked the beginning of a powerful partnership.

I remember my first session at Semicolon Africa. As I stood before the young people, I saw my younger self in them - bright, passionate, and eager to make headway in life. However, what truly made this experience a watershed moment for me was the location. Semicolon's main office is in Yaba, Lagos. Sabo Yaba - as we call it - was my stomping ground during my days at the University of Lagos. My father's house in Iwaya was just a short drive from Sabo Yaba. The church I attended with my father, Yaba Baptist Church, was only a few minutes' walk away from where Semicolon's office now stood.

For me to return to Sabo Yaba, but this time as a facilitator and educator, helping young people find their calling, unlock their potential, and develop their gifts for entrepreneurship, felt like the fulfilment of a prophecy waiting to happen. Years earlier, I had walked through local schools, speaking to students, and inspiring them to believe in their dreams and possibilities. Now, I was back in the same place, but this time, as a professor from a world-renowned business school, still doing the same thing -

moulding lives and building nations.

It was a script that I could never have written for myself. Neither could I have envisioned it unfolding in this way. Between 2019 and 2025, over five hundred young people have gone through my classes at Semicolon Africa, and I have seen many of them emerge as impactful leaders, entrepreneurs, and innovators.

In an instant, my work at the University of Reading found deeper purpose and meaning. I recall telling a friend that even if another university offered me more money, I was not sure I would take it, because I doubted that any other institution could offer me this rare opportunity to return to my roots, empower young people, and be part of a transformative mission. The desire to see young people rise and thrive runs in my veins. This has become the foundation for several projects I have designed and led, all of which have resulted in a significant impact on the lives of thousands of young people across West Africa.

A Full Circle of Purpose and Destiny

Looking back, I realize that life moves in seasons, and if we pay attention, we will notice the common threads that weave through our journey. God is always at work, orchestrating events, connecting dots, and aligning paths in ways that are beyond human comprehension.

Had I not experienced Dubai, I may not have developed a vision for urban transformation. Had I not engaged in community research, I may not have found my passion for social innovation.

Had I not pursued service excellence, I may not have gained the global exposure that shaped my leadership journey. Had I not remained committed to mentoring and teaching, I may never have seen my work come full circle in Yaba. Every experience matters. Every seed we plant in service and faithfulness eventually bears fruit.

The journey of purpose and destiny is often like a tapestry, intricately woven with threads of challenges, victories, setbacks, and breakthroughs. If we remain faithful, diligent, and attentive, we will see how God takes all the separate pieces and works them together to form a masterpiece so breathtaking that it leaves the world in awe. This is not just my story—it is a reminder that each of us has a purpose, a mission, and a destiny to fulfil. When we stay committed, obedient, and willing to serve, our full circle moment will come, and we will stand in awe of how far we have come.

Stay faithful. Stay diligent. Stay open to the unfolding masterpiece of your life.

Principles for Discovering Your Purpose

Throughout my journey, particularly from the moment I turned eighteen and immersed myself deeply in transformative books and mentorship, I began to recognize God's unique purpose for my life. Here, distilled from my experiences, are key principles that can guide you on your journey toward discovering your purpose:

1. **Reflect and Observe Patterns in Your Life**

Purpose often emerges through reflection. Take time to observe recurring themes in your life. For me, it was evident in my deep-seated passion for moulding lives and building nations. This wasn't just an abstract ambition, it became the compass guiding my actions and choices.

2. **Understand Your Background as a Clue**

Our upbringing and early experiences profoundly shape us. Witnessing unrealized potential due to a lack of opportunities sparked my passion for empowerment. Pay attention to what deeply moves you, as this often hints at your life's calling.

3. **Embrace the Power of Servant Leadership**

True purpose is rooted in service. Leadership, at its core, is empowering others. I've always believed that real leadership is not about wielding power but about lifting others. Whether mentoring youth or advocating community changes, purpose often manifests in serving others.

4. **Actively Engage Your Community**

Transformation starts by addressing the needs closest to you. My initial engagements in Iwaya showed me the transformative power of intentional, community-focused action. Engage meaningfully where you are, and a greater purpose will reveal itself.

5. **Pursue Excellence as a Lifestyle**

Excellence opens doors and attracts opportunities. My commitment to excellence in academics, research, and service repeatedly paved the way for remarkable breakthroughs, such as my first trip abroad and various community transformation projects.

6. Be Open to Mentorship and Guidance

Your purpose is often clarified through mentorship. Influential figures in my life shaped my perspective significantly. Embrace mentorship, it sharpens your vision and equips you for your journey.

7. Have the Courage to Act

Your purpose is realized through action. Whether leading seminars, conducting research, or speaking at schools, I learned that taking decisive action was essential in realizing my purpose. The courage to act transforms ideas into realities.

8. Serve Generously and Without Immediate Reward

Genuine service doesn't always seek immediate rewards. My service to the Dean and the resulting unexpected reward taught me that purposeful acts often return blessings in unimaginable ways.

9. Remain Humble and Adaptable

Purpose unfolds progressively. My experiences in the UK required humility and adaptability, crucial for growth and fulfilling purpose. Embrace humility; it accelerates your learning and deepens your impact.

10. Trust in Divine Intentionality

God orchestrates our paths with precision. Looking back, every challenge, success, or detour contributed to my destiny. Trust that your life's events are intentional orchestrations, and stay attentive to the unfolding narrative.

In the tapestry of life, each thread of experience, both trials and triumphs, contributes uniquely to the masterpiece of our purpose. Stay faithful, diligent, and open to divine orchestration. When you embrace these principles, your purpose will reveal itself clearly, allowing you to impact lives profoundly and positively shape generations to come.

Wisdom Keys from Chapter 9

1. **Your Exposure Determines Your Vision:** The places you visit, the people you meet, and the experiences you embrace shape your perception of what is possible.

2. **Excellence in Service Opens Doors of Influence:** Every act of service, no matter how small, is an investment in your future.

3. **Purpose is a Journey, Not a Destination:** Life often brings us back full circle—returning us to our roots, but in a transformed capacity. Every step in the journey matters, even when we don't see the full picture yet.

4. **God Orchestrates Our Journey:** Life is like a tapestry, woven together with threads of opportunities, challenges, and unexpected turns. God aligns our steps, ensuring that even setbacks and disappointments work in our favour. Trust the process. Stay committed.

Reflection Questions

1. How has your exposure (people, places, or experiences) shaped your mindset about what is possible for your life? Think about moments when stepping into a new environment expanded your vision. What did it teach you?

2. Where can you serve with excellence today that could open doors for your future? Consider areas in your work, community, or personal life where dedicated service could lead to unexpected opportunities and transformation.

3. Looking back, can you see how God has been orchestrating the different seasons of your life? Are there moments that felt like setbacks but later turned into stepping stones? How can you embrace the unfolding story of your journey with faith and purpose?

CHAPTER TEN

Driven by Legacy

"No one is self-made. We are all helped individuals."

- Adeyinka Adewale

How do I want to be remembered when I'm gone? What kind of impact do I want my life to leave on others? What name will I pass down to future generations? These questions demand deliberate answers.

Legacies don't happen by chance. They're built through intentional living, shaped by discipline, and held together by accountability. The greatest lives weren't defined by solitary genius but by the strength of relationships—by mentors, guides, and trusted voices who helped shape a life of purpose. No matter how talented, smart, or driven someone is, no one rises alone. Behind every meaningful success is a network—a system of people, principles, and checks that guide, correct, and elevate.

The world applauds pioneers and history-makers, but we often miss the quiet forces behind them, the mentors, teachers, pastors, parents, and coaches who challenged them, refined them and held them to higher standards. Even Jesus, the most influential leader in history, didn't walk alone. He chose disciples, listened to counsel, and stayed aligned with the mission His Father gave Him. If even He embraced the need for relationship and accountability, how much more should we?

Every legacy worth building stands on the foundation of accountability. It's what keeps us rooted in purpose, grounded in integrity, and growing in wisdom. Without it, even the most gifted can go astray. History is filled with talented people who didn't fall for lack of skill but for lack of guidance, correction, and submission to something greater than themselves. Proverbs 11:14 (NIV) says it clearly: "For lack of guidance a nation falls, but victory is won through many advisers." Over the years, I've come to see how God places people in our lives to shape our journey, some to mentor us, some to challenge us, and others to refine us through struggle. The relationships we invest in, and the accountability we accept, don't just shape our success, they define our legacy.

To live with legacy in mind is to understand that life is about more than personal wins. It takes humility to learn, courage to be corrected, and wisdom to stay accountable. It means acknowledging that we've all been helped, that we're shaped by those who came before us, and we're responsible to those who'll come after.

As you reach this final chapter, I encourage you to reflect on your systems of accountability. Who speaks into your life? Who sharpens you? Who holds you to your highest standard? These answers will shape whether your life ends up merely successful—or truly significant. I want to end by honouring two women who have been pillars in my journey—my mother and my wife. Their presence has guided and protected me more than words can express. Others have also been part of my inner circle, but this chapter belongs to these extraordinary women God placed in my life.

The Strength of My Mother

As much as I've spoken about the pivotal role my father played in shaping my life, I've said far less about my mother's quiet but powerful influence. Now it's time to give her the recognition she deserves for the lessons she passed down without knowing, and for the strength she showed every single day. I've never seen resilience like hers.

She overcame odds that would have broken most. With only an elementary education and no way to continue her schooling, she had to build a life from scratch. She grabbed every opportunity she could find. She became one of the very few female barbers in Ibadan from 1968 to 1980, running a successful barbing business. In a time when female barbers were virtually unheard of, she not only built a thriving business but also attracted high-profile clients. More than that, she shared what she knew by training and mentoring other women in the craft.

Today, as an academic who studies female entrepreneurship, I have an even deeper appreciation for what she achieved. The challenges women face in business then and now are staggering. Yet my mother defied expectations, shattered norms, and carved out her path. After her years as a barber, she had reinvented herself, this time as a restaurateur. Her restaurant had a full dining hall, neatly arranged tables and chairs, and a steady stream of loyal customers. As a child, I remember the setting and how busy it was throughout the day. Her restaurant became known for its rich menu and mouthwatering variety, drawing people from all walks of life. From 1980 to 1990, she ran that business with excellence.

This was the woman I woke up to every day: a resilient, hardworking force who kept going, no matter what. She was fearless, disciplined, and relentless in her pursuit of a better life. And she was fiercely protective. One memory still burns bright. One afternoon in school, during the scramble to return to class after lunch, I accidentally stepped on a classmate's kite. It was an honest mistake, but the teacher flogged me so severely it left marks on my back. When I got home and showed my mother, she was furious. The next morning, she marched into my school, found the teacher, and "handled" the situation. I won't share the details, but from that day on, he and every other teacher treated me with a new level of respect.

Looking back, I see that everything my father preached about discipline and hard work, my mother lived out in real-time. She didn't just speak about perseverance, she embodied it. Her life is a lesson in grit, resourcefulness, and quiet strength. I will always be grateful to have been raised by such an extraordinary woman.

Her life shaped mine, and her example continues to inspire me every single day.

The Gift of Number 10

From a young age, I often found myself imagining the woman I would one day marry, how she'd look, who she'd be, and how our lives would intertwine. The idea of finding the right life partner excited me, but I also understood the weight of the choice. Few decisions in life carry more significance. Get it right, and life becomes a journey of purpose and joy. Get it wrong, and life can feel like a constant battle.

The Bible describes a wife as a help meet—a partner, suitable and aligned with her husband (Genesis 2:18). A good woman is more than a companion; she's a supporter of vision and a source of stability. I knew that to fully walk in my purpose, marriage couldn't be left to chance. It had to be divinely guided. I wasn't willing to make a costly mistake, but I also refused to be paralyzed by fear. The answer was simple: watch and pray. And that's exactly what I did.

Once I sensed that I had entered my season of marriage, I turned to prayer. I took deliberate steps to seek God's direction. One of the most defining routines was one a friend and I committed to: every Saturday night, from 10 PM to 11 PM, we prayed specifically for our future homes. For months, we spoke life over marriages that hadn't yet begun. Those prayers would shape my future in ways I couldn't have predicted.

Another pivotal moment came after a Tuesday Bible Study at the University of Reading. I had just finished leading the session and was walking back with two Christian brothers. We stopped by a residence hall for a quick meal, but what began as a casual conversation turned into an all-night prayer meeting. We started at 9 PM and didn't stop until 5 AM. At around 4:30 AM, God spoke through one of the brothers with a prophetic word concerning my marital destiny, full of wisdom, knowledge, and clarity. That night, I knew without question that God had taken the lead.

Soon after, my faith was tested. For three years, I had kept a detailed list of the traits and virtues I wanted in a wife. I regularly reviewed and refined it, treating it like a personal blueprint. Then one evening, while praying, I heard God speak clearly: "Delete the list." I was stunned. Wasn't I just applying biblical wisdom writing the vision and making it plain? Why would God ask me to discard something so intentional? But the instruction grew louder in my spirit. I knew this was a test of trust.

Did I believe that God knew better than I did? Would I allow Him to lead, or would I try to control the outcome?

That night, I deleted the list with these three truths settled in my heart:

- God loves me more than I love myself. No matter how thoughtful my list was, His plan would always be better.

- My vision was limited to my current season. I was picking based on what I thought I needed now. But God knew the full picture—my now and my next.

- God does the heavy lifting. In Genesis, it was God who determined Adam's season, created Eve, brought her to him, and all Adam had to do was recognize her. If that's how the first marriage worked, why should mine be any different?

With a clean slate and a surrendered heart, I trusted God to lead me. Then I met Oluwabamike.

A few months later, our friendship began and gradually grew into the marriage we now share. On the second occasion we met in person, after agreeing to meet at Wimbledon Centre Court Shopping Centre, something unshakable happened. As she walked toward me, I looked at her and thought, *"This is my wife"*.

I just knew. I can't fully explain it. It was an inner confirmation, a peace I couldn't manufacture. I called my spiritual father, Rev Sam Oye, and my pastors in Reading, to share what I had experienced. They prayed with me and offered guidance. A few days later, I got the blessings of all my pastors. Once I was sure this was God's direction, I called my mother to tell her. I did not make the move to formally inform my family until I had become certain this was God's plan for me.

Somewhere in that process, I discovered a beautiful detail that Oluwabamike is the 10th daughter of Francis' Angels. Through her, I gained nine incredible sisters and a second mother. My mother-in-law and sisters-in-law became part of God's gift to me. When I met them, it felt like they had been in my life for decades.

My wife is a divine gift, and within her are strengths, abilities, and qualities that continue to bless, shape, and stabilize my life. Since the day Banks as I affectionately call her came into my life, she has brought calm, balance, and peace. She has been the steadying force in many areas of my life. Ask anyone close to me, and they will tell you I often say: "My wife's financial wisdom saved me from financial foolishness." She challenged my approach to money and helped me make better financial decisions, which, in turn, made me a better man.

When I started pastoring The Transforming Church, she stood beside me, supporting and strengthening me. Because of her, I can pastor with peace of mind. As I travel around the world fulfilling my assignments, she holds the home front with grace. Looking back at the seasons we've walked through, I see the power of God's choice. If I had followed my way, I wouldn't be here today. She is the testimony of God's faithfulness in my life.

Through her, God has blessed us with two amazing children, ImisiOluwa and IniOluwa. And for their sake, I have made a covenant with God: to live a life worthy of emulation and to leave them a legacy that will outlive me.

A great marriage is not about finding a "perfect person", it is about finding the one whom God has made perfect for you. In Banke, I found that person, and every day, I remain grateful that I trusted God with this decision.

Accountability: A Key to Building a Lasting Legacy

Purpose doesn't thrive in isolation—it's shaped, refined, and sustained through accountability. This structure helps sharpen our focus, keep our values intact, and ensure we stay aligned with our calling. Talent, vision, and discipline are essential, but without accountability, even the strongest can lose direction.

One of the greatest gifts of accountability is the people it brings into our lives—those who challenge, support and strengthen us. They help us see what we often miss, push us beyond our assumptions, and offer wisdom where we lack it. These are the voices that steady our steps and the hands that help us build on solid ground.

God places different types of accountability relationships in our lives, each with a unique role. Recognizing and embracing them is key to walking in wisdom and leaving a lasting legacy:

- **The Guiding Hands (Mentors, Coaches, and Pastors):** These are people who've gone before us. They carry the scars of experience and the wisdom that comes with time. Their insight helps us avoid costly mistakes and make better decisions. As Proverbs 15:22 (NIV) reminds us, "Plans fail for lack of counsel, but with many advisers they succeed."

- **The Loving Anchors (Family and Trusted Friends):** These are the mirrors in our lives—our spouses, families, and close friends who reflect our strengths and weaknesses to us. They remind us who we are, keep us grounded, and stand with us through every season.

- **The Iron Sharpeners (Peers and Accountability Partners):** Like iron sharpening iron, these people push us to grow. They ask the hard questions, hold us to our word, and challenge us not to settle for less than our best.

- **The Divine Connection (God's Role in Accountability):** At the centre of it all is God—the ultimate source of guidance and correction. Submitting to His leadership keeps us from drifting into self-reliance. He aligns our path, brings the right people at the right time, and ensures we never walk alone.

Accountability is a gift. It protects purpose, sustains momentum, and builds a foundation that legacy can stand on. The people God places around us aren't just for companionship; they are part of His design to help us finish well. When we embrace accountability—through mentors, peers, loved ones, and above all, divine guidance—we don't just succeed, we grow in wisdom, character, and impact. If legacy is the goal, accountability is the path. Walk it boldly.

Legacy is not about the wealth we accumulate or the accolades we receive. It is about the lives we impact and the values we pass on to future generations. As I reflect on my journey, I realize that legacy is sustained through the systems of accountability we submit to. Without them, we are vulnerable to distractions, errors, and detours that can rob us of our purpose.

Through my mother, I saw the power of resilience and tenacity, the ability to push through adversity and build something out of nothing. Through my wife, I learned the power of alignment, and support, and how the right partner can bring stability, wisdom, and peace. Through my mentors, pastors, and friends, I experienced the power of counsel, refinement, and how being surrounded by the right voices can propel one toward destiny. I have remained submissive to these systems as I yet continue in life's journey.

As I bring *The Wisdom of 40 Summers* to a close, I leave you with this thought: You are a product of the people you listen to, the systems you submit to, and the accountability you embrace.

You are not here by accident. You were designed to impact lives, influence generations, and leave a mark that outlives you. But to do this, you must build wisely, surround yourself with the right people, and never walk alone.

Let this be your commitment: To live intentionally, to remain accountable, and to build a legacy that speaks long after you are gone.

Wisdom Keys from Chapter 10

1. **No One is Self-Made, We Are All Helped Individuals:** Every great person has been shaped by the influence, mentorship, and support of others. True greatness is recognizing and embracing those whom God has sent to help you.

2. **Accountability is the Backbone of a Lasting Legacy:** Without systems of accountability—mentors, peers, family, and spiritual leaders—even the most talented individuals can stray from their purpose. Seek guidance, remain teachable, and stay grounded.

3. **The Right Relationships Are Legacy Catalysts:** The right people in your life will challenge you, correct you, and help you grow. Do not just seek comfort; seek relationships that sharpen you into the best version of yourself.

4. **Legacy is Not What You Leave For People, But What You Leave In People:** Wealth and accomplishments may fade, but the wisdom, values, and impact you deposit into others will outlive you. Live in a way that ensures your influence continues for generations.

Reflection Questions

1. Who are the key accountability partners in your life, and how do they help you grow?

2. What kind of legacy are you building today? How do you want to be remembered?

3. What changes do you need to make to ensure you are submitting to the right systems of accountability that will help you fulfil your purpose?

Now, go forth, live wisely, and build a legacy that will stand the test of time. The best is yet to come.

The Wisdom of 40 Summers: Stories Of Grace, Grit And Growth

1. **Circumstances Do Not Define Us, Our Choices Do**
While we do not choose the families or conditions we are born into, we have the power to shape our lives through the choices we make. My journey illustrates that even in complex family dynamics, one can rise above challenges through intentional choices.

2. **Perspective Determines Reality**
The shift in mindset from focusing on limitations to embracing possibilities was a turning point. A change in perspective, choosing to see every experience as a contributor to growth, can redefine our lives and open doors to greater opportunities.

3. **Adversity is a Catalyst for Growth**
The discomfort of leaving a familiar environment and adapting to new circumstances became the foundation for transformation. Growth often requires stepping out of our comfort zones and embracing the unknown with courage.

4. **The Power of Thought Shapes Destiny**
The lesson from As a Man Thinketh and Gifted Hands revealed that thoughts dictate outcomes. The decision to envision a brighter future, despite past difficulties, led to a renewed sense of purpose and ambition. As James Allen puts it, "You are today where your thoughts have brought you; you will be tomorrow where your thoughts take you."

5. **Timing is Everything**
Just like the concrete caps needed to be stamped at the right moment, not too soon and not too late, opportunities in life also have optimal timing. Acting at the right time can yield the best

results, while hesitation or delay can make progress much harder or even impossible.

6. Diligence is a Pathway to Excellence

The rigorous discipline instilled by my father, from household chores to academic rigour, proved invaluable in shaping a strong work ethic. Excellence is rarely accidental; it is a product of consistent diligence and commitment to doing things well.

7. Success happens when Preparation Meets Opportunity

The unexpected Pythagoras theorem test proved that preparation can transform luck into success. What seemed like a random study session turned out to be the very key to winning a scholarship. Success often comes to those who prepare even when they don't see immediate results.

8. Hard Work Outlasts Talent

While talent provides an advantage, discipline and hard work are what sustain success. Just like elite athletes who put in extra effort behind the scenes, those who commit to mastering their craft will eventually outshine those who rely on talent alone.

9. Consistency Sustains Excellence

Achievements are not just about talent or past victories; they require continuous discipline and effort. Letting go of the habits that brought success can quickly lead to setbacks.

10. Humility is the Foundation of Growth

Success can create a false sense of invincibility, but life has a way of humbling even the most accomplished. Staying teachable and disciplined is key to sustained success.

11. Failure is a Pathway, Not a Destination

Facing multiple failures in a short period can be disheartening, but perseverance through disappointment strengthens character and prepares you for bigger victories.

12. Success has Unconventional Paths

Sometimes, the road to your goals is not a straight line. Detours, delays, and unexpected opportunities—like the University of Lagos Diploma program—can still lead to success if you remain open to new possibilities.

13. Your Circle Is Your Catalyst

Who you surround yourself with determines the trajectory of your life. Mentors, friends, and associates can either elevate your potential or hinder your growth. Choose your circle wisely.

14. Proximity to Greatness Inspires Greatness

Being in the presence of visionary thinkers, mentors, and positive role models ignites ambition and expands your perspective. Seeking out and learning from accomplished individuals accelerates personal and professional growth.

15. Giving Opens the Doors to Greater Blessings

True success is not just about personal achievement but also about impacting others. The act of selfless giving, as seen in providing scholarships, often unlocks unexpected rewards and divine favour.

16. The Right Voices Reveal the Right Opportunities

Sometimes, all it takes is one conversation, one lecture, or one book recommendation to shift your path. When you're surrounded by wise voices, you see doors you didn't know existed.

17. Opportunities Often Come Disguised as Challenges

Life-changing moments don't always appear as grand invitations. Sometimes, they come in the form of unexpected tests, intimidating challenges, or moments of uncertainty. Recognizing these disguised opportunities is key to unlocking success.

18. Courage to Try Is the First Step to Success

Fear of failure stops many from seizing life-changing opportunities. The willingness to step out, even when uncertain of the outcome, often leads to incredible growth, unexpected victories, and new paths you never imagined.

19. Failure to Act often births Regret

In the long run, we often regret the chances we didn't take more than the mistakes we made. Even when things don't go as planned, taking action always leads to growth, experience, and new doors opening.

20. Every Experience Contributes to Your Future

No moment in life is wasted. Even seemingly insignificant experiences—helping in a family business, past failures, or minor academic struggles—often prepare you for success in ways you don't realize until much later.

21. Success is a Launchpad, Not a Destination

Every win expands your vision and opens doors to greater

possibilities. Instead of seeing success as a finish line, view it as a stepping stone to something even bigger.

22. Entrepreneurship is First a Mindset

Opportunity often comes disguised as a challenge. How we see them determines the outcome we get. Those who take action, adapt, and collaborate will always find ways to create value and grow.

23. Partnerships Unlock Resources and Multiply Impact

The right partnerships and strategic collaborations provide access to resources, knowledge, and opportunities that one cannot achieve alone. Identifying and working with the right people at the right time can accelerate your success.

24. Bold Action Turns Ordinary Moments Into Opportunity

Opportunities rarely announce themselves. It's your willingness to act that reveals them. Trusting in God is essential, but faith must be accompanied by bold steps and sacrifice. When we act on our faith, we position ourselves for divine breakthroughs and limitless growth.

25. Every Challenge is a Refining Process

Like a blacksmith's fire purifies metal, life's trials are not meant to break us but to shape us. Hardships are not punishments; they are preparation for a greater calling.

26. Crisis Moments Reveal New Terrains

Difficult seasons introduce us to unfamiliar challenges some expose our weaknesses, some test our patience, and others prepare us for transitions. How we navigate them determines our growth.

27. Service and Submission Unlock Unexpected Blessings

True growth happens when we humble ourselves to serve others. Serving with sincerity whether in leadership, faith, or friendships opens doors we never imagined and accelerates our spiritual and personal development.

28. God's Preparation is Always Ahead of Your Next Season

Before every major transition, God places us in a "training ground" to equip us for what's ahead. Recognizing and embracing these seasons of preparation allows us to step into new opportunities fully prepared.

29. Seasons of Pain are Doors to a Greater Purpose

Life's darkest moments are often the training grounds for greater assignments. Just as my faith was strengthened through hardships, our trials are not pointless; they refine and prepare us for bigger responsibilities in the future.

30. Obedience to God Unlocks Unexpected Blessings

Sacrifices made in obedience to God are never wasted. The seed sown in faith—whether time, resources, or service—eventually returns in multiplied blessings.

31. Serving in the Waiting Season Brings Clarity and Breakthrough

In seasons of uncertainty, it is easy to feel stuck. However, rather than staying idle or discouraged, choosing to serve can be the key to unlocking the next phase of life. Even when faced with uncertainty about the future, I poured myself into service, and in doing so, God aligned my steps.

32. God's Preparation is Intentional

Every challenge, success, and experience in life is a piece of God's grand design. He equips us with the strength, faith, and resilience needed for future challenges. Nothing is random; God is always working behind the scenes, shaping us for what lies ahead.

33. Your Exposure Determines Your Vision

The places you visit, the people you meet, and the experiences you embrace shape your perception of what is possible.

34. Excellence in Service Opens Doors of Influence

Every act of service, no matter how small, is an investment in your future.

35. Purpose is a Journey, Not a Destination

Life often brings us back full circle—returning us to our roots, but in a transformed capacity. Every step in the journey matters, even when we don't see the full picture yet.

36. God Orchestrates Our Journey

Life is like a tapestry, woven together with threads of opportunities, challenges, and unexpected turns. God aligns our steps, ensuring that even setbacks and disappointments work in our favour. Trust the process. Stay committed.

37. No One is Self-Made, We Are All Helped Individuals

Every great person has been shaped by the influence,

mentorship, and support of others. True greatness is recognizing and embracing those whom God has sent to help you.

38. Accountability is the Backbone of a Lasting Legacy
Without systems of accountability, mentors, peers, family, and spiritual leaders, even the most talented individuals can stray from their purpose. Seek guidance, remain teachable, and stay grounded.

39. The Right Relationships Are Legacy Catalysts
The right people in your life will challenge you, correct you, and help you grow. Do not just seek comfort; seek relationships that sharpen you into the best version of yourself.

40. Legacy is Not What You Leave For People, But What You Leave In People
Wealth and accomplishments may fade, but the wisdom, values, and impact you deposit into others will outlive you. Live in a way that ensures your influence continues for generations.

ABOUT THE AUTHOR

Dr. Adeyinka Adewale is an Associate Professor of Leadership Ethics and Entrepreneurship at Henley Business School, University of Reading, UK, where he also leads the Africa Research Centre. He is a respected voice in the global leadership and ethics space — known for his award-winning research on character, virtue, and the moral pressures leaders face in complex environments. A sought-after speaker and consultant, Adeyinka has delivered keynote addresses across Europe, Africa, and beyond, engaging with leaders in government, business, and civil society. His work has influenced policy discussions at the European Union and shaped international thinking on leadership, governance, and ethical development in Africa.

In addition to his academic and advisory roles, Adeyinka serves as a pastor at The Transforming Church UK, where he continues to disciple public leaders and actively engage organisations and communities with the message of hope, purpose, and transformation. His work at the intersection of faith and leadership reflects a lifelong commitment to raising people of influence who lead with integrity and spiritual depth. He also serves on the boards of innovative start-ups and purpose-driven charities across continents. His writing, teaching, and ministry are all grounded in one passion: helping people and institutions lead with clarity, conviction, and character.

www.ingramcontent.com/pod-product-compliance
Lightning Source LLC
Chambersburg PA
CBHW030454100526
44580CB00010B/130/J